6/07

DISCARD

THE FIRST-TIME MANAGER'S GUIDE TO

TEAM BUILDING

Gary S. Topchik

D0113332

ΛMACOM

American Management Association
New York • Atlanta • Brussels • Chicago • Mexico City • San Francisco
Shanghai • Tokyo • Toronto • Washington, D. C.

Special discounts on bulk quantities of AMACOM books are available to corporations, professional associations, and other organizations. For details, contact Special Sales Department, AMACOM, a division of American Management Association, 1601 Broadway, New York, NY 10019.
Tel.: 212-903-8316. Fax: 212-903-8083.
Website: www.amacombooks.org

This publication is designed to provide accurate and authoritative information in regard to the subject matter covered. It is sold with the understanding that the publisher is not engaged in rendering legal, accounting, or other professional service. If legal advice or other expert assistance is required, the services of a competent professional person should be sought.

Library of Congress Cataloging-in-Publication Data

Topchik, Gary S.
    The first-time manager's guide to team building / Gary S. Topchik.
        p.   cm.
    Includes index.
    ISBN-13: 978-0-8144-7429-7
    ISBN-10: 0-8144-7429-2
    1. Executives—Training of.   2. Leadership—Study and teaching.   3. Teams in the workplace.   4. Interpersonal communication.   5. Employee motivation.   I. Title.
    HD30.4.T67   2007
    658.4'022—dc22   2007007104

Printing number

10   9   8   7   6   5   4   3   2   1

Contents

Acknowledgments

Our teams at work make us look good and help us to succeed. I have had great teams supporting me during the writing of this book. I would like to extend my sincere thanks to the team at AMACOM, especially Adrienne Hickey, editorial director. This is the fourth book that AMACOM and I have collaborated on, and I am honored to be part of the team.

I would also like to thank my team at home for supporting me and encouraging me to write another book. Then there is Alexandra and her team at USC. I owe them a tremendous amount of thanks. There is also the village of Eygaliers to thank. I met the most wonderful people there during the writing of this book. They were a true inspiration. Last, I need to recognize all the great managers in the many different organizations I have worked and consulted in during the last many years. They are the ones who have shown me, through their incredible management and leadership skills, what it really takes to build a team.

—GST

Introduction

There are a lot of managers out there who have not realized the great advantages of team building. They see themselves rather than their team members as the focal point, the most knowledgeable, and the decision maker. This book does not buy into that philosophy. Its major goal is to show you how high-performing teams can be a tremendous advantage to the team manager or team builder, the team members themselves, and to your organization.

The First-Time Manager's Guide to Team Building will tell you how to create and maintain a high-powered, results-oriented team that will get the job done. You will develop the skills needed to become a successful manager of teams and discover innovative ways to make your teams more productive. *The First-Time Manager's Guide to Team Building* begins with a description of what a team is, compares the four different team models, and tells you how you can get your team to the highest levels of team performance. It then tells you how you can successfully go from being an individual contributor to a manager of teams by developing a new set of skills and avoiding the roadblocks along the way. Then it leads you through the critical 10 steps to team building. These steps, if followed, guarantee immediate success in your team-building efforts.

The book then tells you how you can build team spirit by focusing on the five competencies that all high-performing teams possess: clear roles and responsibilities; open, honest communication; a supportive, knowledgeable team leader or manager; decision-making authority; and rewards and recognition. You will also learn many new strategies for managing challenging team situations, such as how to hold teams and team members accountable, deal with difficult team personalities, and move your teams from conflict to collaboration. The book also contains many team-building activities such as The Original Game, The Unsighted Square, and Team Temperature. These activities develop a team environment and a team culture, enabling a team to perform at the highest level possible. The book concludes with how you can use class to build your teams.

The First-Time Manager's Guide to Team Building is written in a conversational manner, making it easy for you to follow along and absorb the ideas. There are many practical examples and case studies that highlight the points being made. You'll find it easy to refer back to specific areas when specific concerns arise in the future. I highly recommend that you reread the book several months after you have started building your teams. And please share the book with your colleagues so they will be able to build their teams as well.

The First-Time Manager's Guide to Team Building is also extremely valuable for experienced managers of teams. It will remind them of what they used to do, which they may need to do again, or will confirm whether what they are currently doing is on the mark. But our focus will be on the first-time manager or team leader.

There are many books on the subject of team building, but few of them focus on individuals such as you—new to managing and new to building a team. First-time managers are not interested in a lot of theories and studies; they want to focus on the practicalities of developing a team that performs well. That is what we will zero in on in this book.

My major purpose in writing this book was to give you great satisfaction from building your teams. Thanks for spending some time with *The First-Time Manager's Guide to Team Building*.

• PART ONE •

The Team

The Best Team Experience

I often begin my team-building sessions and seminars with a great exercise that pinpoints what makes for a really good team. I give the individuals present (who consist mostly of current managers and team leaders or those about to move into these roles) the following task: Think of the best team you have ever worked on, or currently work on, or unfortunately, if neither applies, could imagine working on.

A minute or two later, after they have thought about the assignment, I ask them this question: What about that team made it, makes it, or in your fantasy, would make it such a great team?

I usually get a great quantity of answers, and the answers always correlate to what first-time managers need to do to build their own high-performing teams. There are certain characteristics and behaviors that get repeated time after time. The list often looks like this.

Characteristics and Behaviors of the Best Team Experiences

- The right people on the team
- A great team leader or manager who really cares about the team
- Fun—enjoyment of the people and the team experience
- Enjoyment of the work the team is responsible for

- Clearly defined common goal or goals
- Ways to measure successes or results
- Accomplishment of team goal(s)
- Celebration of successes
- Rewards and recognition when goals are met or exceeded
- Performance accountability
- Clearly defined roles and responsibilities for each team member
- Strategies for handling challenging team members
- Ability to make decisions freely
- Clear directions and specific time frames
- Availability of the resources needed for success
- Open and honest communication among team members and between the manager and the team
- A team leader or manager who works across department lines to get what is needed for her team
- A vision of how the goals of the team tie in to organizational goals
- Mutual support among team members
- A team leader who teaches the members how to work as a team
- Interdependence

When I ask my seminar group members what specific teams they were thinking of when I asked them to think of their best team experiences, I get a huge variety of answers. It seems that these best team experiences exist in every type of industry, in both for-profit or nonprofit organizations, in governmental agencies, and in every part of the world. Sometimes they are sports teams or community-based teams.

Here are two sad notes that I must report, however, about this best-team exercise. First, about 20 percent of the responses to my initial question have to do with a fantasy team. Unfortunately, there are many managers and team leaders who have not had any best-team experience. I hope that will change when they manage their own teams! Second, more people have had bad team experiences than positive ones, and they have had more bad team leaders and managers than good ones. It is also interesting to note that when I ask the opposite question (as I sometimes do), "Think of the worst team experiences," I get the opposite answers to the Characteristics and Behaviors of the Best Team Experiences list.

Building Team Spirit

The definition of team spirit is pretty close to the definition of a team. Team spirit is the willingness and the ability to work in an interdependent fashion where any team member needs to rely on other team members to accomplish the work or the goals of the team. Over the years I have taken this best-team experience exercise one step further. I have asked thousands to select five items from the Characteristics and Behaviors of the Best Team Experiences list that they think are the most important or have the highest priority for building a team. Consistently, I get these five, but not in any particular order:

1. Clearly defined roles and responsibilities for each team member
2. Open and honest communication among team members and between the manager and the team
3. A supportive and knowledgeable manager/leader
4. Ability to make decisions freely
5. Rewards and recognition when goals are met or exceeded

These five are among the most important elements to building a team spirit, which, in turn builds a high-performing team.

So a very important question for first-time managers or experienced managers to ask themselves is: Are these five characteristics of team spirit prevalent in my teams? If they are not, what can I do to make sure they are?

2

Defining a Team

Defining a Team

Teams are groups of individuals who accomplish designated objectives by working interdependently, communicating effectively, and making decisions that affect their work. They often have a certain level of autonomy and they develop procedures for accomplishing their goals. Ongoing training in both technical and team skills are also a hallmark of a team, as is the team leader or manager getting training on how to manage and lead a team.

Teams have a common purpose or goal and a clear mission statement of that purpose. They know what their desired results are and they can measure their progress toward those goals. A team's goals are aligned with the goals of the department and/or organization, and team members have a very clear understanding and appreciation for how their efforts meet the broader goals of the organization.

Team Size

There is no ideal team size, but in general (and there are always many exceptions) most successful workplace teams tend to have between five and 10 people. When a team is too small, there are not enough people to get the work done. When the team gets too large, communication and decision making are difficult. Imagine a group of 12 or 15 of your friends trying to decide where to have dinner. The same thing happens in teams that are too large when they need to have decision-making discussions. Larger teams tend to divide naturally or are purposely divided into smaller groups or subteams. This increases the time it takes to communicate, make decisions, and get the job done.

Ongoing Teams and Project Teams

There are two major types of teams: the ongoing team and the project team. The members of an ongoing team stay together indefinitely. People who work in the same department or unit, such as a manager and her staff, are an example of an ongoing team. In most companies you will have many ongoing teams such as the IT team, the marketing-research team, and the accounts payable team.

Project teams, on the other hand, are formed for a particular purpose. They usually disband when their mission is accomplished. Often project teams are cross-functional; that is, the group members come from different functional areas in the organization. For example, if an organization wanted to improve work flow among five different departments, the team members would probably come from each of these five departments as well as from other areas of the company such as engineering, human resources, or organizational change and development.

Ongoing teams usually have team members with the same status or title, except for the manager, who is a level above. This is often quite different on project teams. I have seen project teams composed of individuals at many different levels. It would not be unusual to have a couple of vice presidents on a team with others who are two or three levels below in title. I always find these mixtures fascinating. I have seen programmers or research scientists, for example, advising senior managers on what has to be done. Because these senior managers do not know as much about particular technical issues, they have to rely on their team members. That is what a team should be all about. Knowledge and experience should be valued more than titles.

So Many Benefits

There are countless benefits to having teams or a team-based organization. Let me just mention a few. First, most people prefer working on teams, and if given the opportunity to do so, will perform better. Second, individuals on teams find their work more meaningful and rewarding than those not on teams. Third, teams enable organizations to use their people—their number-one resource—better, thereby getting much higher returns on their investments in teams. Fourth, many teams become so effective that they can work without direct management support. This sense of autonomy is an incredible motivator for many team members. Fifth, sometimes a team can become so effective that it makes up for the fact that the team's manager is ineffective. Sixth, teams have the power of synergy; it is a proven fact that teams generally make better decisions than individuals. This results in more-innovative, better solutions to problems. All in all, these are some very strong reasons for having teams.

Who Should the Team Leader Be?

Some organizations put a subject-matter expert (SME) in charge of a team—someone who has the technical knowledge but not necessarily the team-leadership skills. By team-leadership skills I mean the ability to communicate well, motivate people, facilitate discussions, make decisions, resolve conflicts, listen, deal with difficult team members, etc. A big mistake that these organizations often make is relying on the person's technical skills to lead and manage a team. They definitely are not enough. It is just as important, and sometimes even more important, for the manager to have great team skills as well.

The same holds for first-time managers who may have been promoted for their technical skills and not their team skills. Just because they were good technically does not mean that they will be good team leaders or builders of teams.

A developing trend in many organizations today is to assign or hire individuals with great managerial, leadership, and team skills and have them acquire the technical knowledge over time. Generally, I think it is a fine approach. However, the organizational culture and the team members must value these skills and not believe that the only way one can be a very good team manager or leader is to be as technically proficient or more technically proficient than their team members.

Who Should the Team Members Be?

The opposite of what I just said about team leaders holds true for team members. When forming a team, especially a project team, the individuals' skills, knowledge, and experience should be the number-one criteria for team membership. Then it is the responsibility of the manager, team leader, or organization to help develop each member's team skills through team-building training programs. Never put people on a team just because they like one another, get along with each other, have similar personalities, or because you want a mix of different personalities. This approach will most likely backfire.

Here's a true story that brings out the point. I was once working in a company where the CEO had just returned from a two-week executive leadership program. As part of the program, he was exposed to a particular personality instrument and immediately became a devotee of it. When he returned to his company, he had each employee (about 300) take the instrument. Then he reorganized all of the teams so that each had at least one person of each personality style or type on it. The CEO's strategy turned out to be a disaster. Many of the teams no longer had the SMEs needed to perform the work even though they had a nice mix of personality and behavioral styles. Productivity and profitability soon dropped.

I do not want to give the impression that other factors beside subject-matter expertise are irrelevant when hiring individuals or assigning them to teams. Other factors, especially experience working on teams and attitude toward teams are vital. I am just saying, once again—and this is a key point—that knowledge, expertise, and ability in the team's subject matter should be the top priority. You should definitely ask certain questions before hiring staff members or putting them on a team. If someone says he would rather work alone or that she does not see the value of teamwork, then, if you have a choice, don't put that person on a team or employ them in a company that values teams.

Are You Really Managing a Team?

A group of people working together is not necessarily a team if it does not fit the definition of what a team is—especially the key part about working interdependently. Often people in the same work group, unit, department, etc., call themselves a team even though their interactions do not match the definition of a team. Developing a team, in the true sense of the word, is very hard work and the responsibility lies with the organization, the team manager or leader, and the team members themselves.

3

The Four Team Models

There are four different ways you can structure, organize, and manage your teams. These four ways, or team models, have different communication and decision-making styles. As a first-time manager, you need to decide which model best fits the people you manage, the nature of their work, and the culture of your organization. Before we look at the four team models, let's briefly discuss the three factors that determine the best way to set up a team.

The Three Factors of Team Life

There are three major factors that you should consider when deciding on how you need to structure you team's communication and decision making. The first and most important factor is the current subject-matter expertise of your team members. Are they highly, moderately, or not technically skilled? To what degree can they learn and develop? Can they work on their own and interdependently with others, or do they need lots of direction and training from you? You also need to look at their current level of team skills, sometimes called interpersonal skills. Are they able to communicate effectively with one another, listen to different points of view, motivate one another, come up with a consensus decision, and deal with team members who challenge the group process or do not do their part? Or do you have to take the lead in all or most of these areas?

The second factor of team life is the nature of the team's work. Some types of work lend themselves more to one type of team model then another. For example, in some work environments, each team member may have a specific job to do independently. Or, because of the nature of the work, each team member may have to make his or her own decisions without consulting any of the team members. In other work environments, the opposite would be true: in order to reach a goal the team member needs to work with others or needs the help and assistance of others. This is where interdependence comes in.

The last factor to think about before deciding which team model would be best for you is the culture of your organization or department. Some organizations or departments encourage two-way communication between managers and their team members. They want managers to ask team members for their thoughts and opinions, and they respect and value those opinions. They view their team members as having an integral part in determining what needs to be done in order for the team to succeed.

Other organizations communicate in a top-down fashion, where managers make the decisions. In these cultures team members are expected to do their work and do it well, but they are not expected to get involved in much decision making. The managers like to run the show, and that message is constantly communicated to their team members. Obviously, there are many organizations that lay somewhere along this continuum, from more-participative work environments to more-controlling ones.

A big part of being able to work well within your organization's culture is to take into account your direct manager's philosophy and beliefs about teams. Often he or she may have a somewhat different approach than the organization's. You need to be very cognizant of that. In order for you to succeed in your new role, you will need to know what your manager expects from you.

The three factors of team life are closely interrelated. You cannot consider one without the other two. Let me give you a very common example of what I mean.

The Case of the Incongruent Factors of Team Life

You have a highly technically skilled team that has mastered team skills as well. The nature of the team's projects calls for the members to work interdependently. So far, I hope, you are thinking that you can have a high-performing team here. You have a team that can basically work on its own with a little direction and support from you.

However, the culture of your organization basically dictates that managers make the decisions and monitor the work of all team members very closely. So what do you do in this case, where there is incongruence among the three factors of team life?

In this example, you would consider the environment you work in. You cannot completely go against the organization's culture if you want to be successful within that organization. However, there may be a way to advocate a different managerial strategy as long as you get the results the organization demands. As the leader of your team you need to try to convince management that what you believe is best for your team would in turn be best for the organization. One of the most difficult aspects of managing people and teams and creating high-performing teams is not having all three factors of team life aligned or congruent.

Which Is the Most Important Factor of the Three?

I am sure that at this stage you are well aware that you have to consider the nature of the work that your team does, the culture of the organization, and the team members' level of subject-matter expertise. However, many first-time managers only focus on the latter. On one hand that could be a big problem, but on the other hand it's the right thing to do. The most important factor in developing a team to its highest possible level of performance is generally your team members' current level of subject-matter expertise. Ideally, that factor, more that the other two, determines the approach you take to team building. But we can definitely not forget about the other two.

Descriptions of the Four Team Models

As you read the descriptions of the four team models, think of the team or teams that you currently lead or will be leading in the future. Which model comes closest to yours? Is it the best model for your team's current situation? Would a different model be more effective? And keep in mind the three factors of team life when deciding which model works best for you.

The Work Group

Dennis is a new manager at a large computer-chip manufacturing company in Austin. He moved into his position a few months ago from another chip company. He inherited a group of six. Dennis had never managed before but looked forward to working with his group.

Dennis assigns each person specific responsibilities and meets separately with each member weekly to monitor progress. He also holds update meetings with his entire group, where he shares new information and answers questions. Dennis makes the decisions, and the group members have come to accept them. So far they have had no complaints. Dennis considers himself to be very successful with his group and enjoys his job as their manager. The group members like one another and there is little conflict among them. However, there is very limited interaction among them during the work day. Each member has his own work products, and work-related communication is almost always only with Dennis. He has asked his management for feedback on how he is doing, and they have all responded favorably.

The Developing Team

Reilly is a new sales manager responsible for a line of industrial products used in the tool and die industry. Her region is the southeastern United States, and she has 10 sales reps reporting directly to her. She was promoted from within the group of sales reps, and her former peers are now her team. It took them several months to get over the change, but they now fully accept Reilly as the boss. Reilly talked with her team members about how they felt about her taking over and how difficult this change must be for them. She also explained how she planned on leading the team and what her expectations were. In order to make this change work, Reilly also had to change her own perspective. She had to identify with being a manager now and could no longer see herself as one of the sales reps.

Each of Reilly's sales reps is responsible for his own geographic area. Reilly communicates with her reps at least two or three times a day to see how they are doing, to avert any potential problems, and to give advice and suggestions. She always listens to their concerns and ideas. Once a month the sales reps and Reilly meet in person. Sometimes, due to scheduling conflicts, not all of the sales reps or Reilly can meet face-to-face. When this occurs, Reilly holds a virtual meeting.

At her meetings, Reilly presents new directives from senior management. She decides before the meeting how to implement these directives, but before she states how she plans on doing it, she asks the reps for their input. If she gets a really good idea that differs from hers, she is willing to change her mind.

The sales reps often help each other out with customer histories and specific sales or customer-service strategies that have worked for them. They do this on their own without involving Reilly.

Reilly has just gotten approval from her VP to hold a team-building session with her sales reps. At these sessions Reilly will talk about what it means to work on a team and the importance of teamwork. She will also help the team members acquire skills that help them rely more on one another and less on her. Reilly is currently getting some outside training in how to lead a team and the dynamics of teamwork.

Reilly believes she is doing well with her team and enjoys her new managerial position. Her team members and VP have given her high marks on the recent 360-degree performance feedback that the company does twice a year.

The Participative Team

Leticia is a first-time manager at a packaging-design consulting company in Seattle. Before coming to Seattle, she worked as a lay-out-design specialist in France. Her current company helps other companies design or redesign the packaging for their products. She manages a team of seven highly skilled and motivated team members who all have had prior team experience.

Leticia and her team meet on a regular basis, usually every day, to discuss and decide on the designs for each of the products they are responsible for. Often her team members disagree with her and with one another. Leticia and each team member listens to each others' arguments and, eventually, they reach a consensus on how to proceed. Leticia's viewpoint has no more weight than the viewpoints of any other team member. She totally trusts their expertise and vice versa. Leticia considers herself to be very successful with her team and enjoys her job as their manager.

The Autonomous Team

For the last few years Paul has been a Web design manager for one of the larger department store chains in the world. In order to make more money and to gain management experience, Paul applied for and landed a job at a small Web-design company in Los Angeles. He got a very big shock when he arrived at his new job.

At his former company, managers basically told their team members what to do. At his new company, he was informed that he was to give just some overall direction and time frames to his team of five and then "be there" if they needed some help or information. It took him some time to adjust to this new type of work environment, but now he feels extremely comfortable in it. He likes this team philosophy. The way teams are structured here enables him to work on his own projects and spend more of his time planning and organizing the work of his team so they can work independently from him and interdependently with one another. He has learned to trust their expertise and decision making.

Previously, most of Paul's day went to giving directions to his team and closely monitoring their work. He never really had time to do anything else. Now he also has the time to help out other teams that may need some of his expertise and take on special projects from above. He even has the time to keep up his own technical expertise.

Paul's team members explained to him that a few years ago they needed much more guidance and support from their manager. But now that they have become more skilled and knowledgeable about what they do and have learned how to solve problems as a team, they enjoy their jobs so much more. His team has been getting the results needed and Paul is very pleased with his decision to change jobs.

Because Dennis, Reilly, Leticia, and Paul all seem to be very successful with their teams, I would have to say that all of the team models work. In chapter 4, we'll take a closer look at all of the models so you can decide which one(s) best fits your three factors of team life. Which team model you decide on, once again, really depends on what you want communication and decision making to be like. Please remember this key point: There is no ideal team model; they all get results—but they get results in different ways. However, I and many others in the field of management and team building would argue that participative and autonomous teams get results that affect the bottom line more than the work group and developing teams do.

• 4 •

A Summary of the Four Models

There are different ways to structure a team, and as I said in chapter 3, no one model is the best model. It all depends on the three factors of team life, especially the team's skill level.

The Work Group

The first of the four models is the work group. The work group does not fit the classic definition of a team. Therefore, technically we will not call it a team. But if the work is getting done and morale and productivity are good, it is a model that is working for you, so keep it.

Characteristics of the Work Group

- One-way communication; top down
- Little work-related communication among group members
- Manager makes the decisions

This model works best when the manager or team leader is the most knowledgeable of the group and when team members are new, inexperienced, or not skilled enough to make decisions. The model also works well when the team members do not have to communicate much with one another in order to get their work done. Additionally, some organizations prefer the manager to be in charge and make all decisions. If this is the type of organization that you work for, you need to consider this model unless you can make the point that another team model would serve the organization better.

But think about this. Perhaps morale, quality of work, productivity, or profitability would be even better with one of the other models. This last sentence assumes that your work group can work more interdependently, the nature of the work lends itself to more of a team environment, and your organization would support teams.

The Developing Team

The developing team begins to fit our definition of what a team truly is.

Characteristics of the Developing Team

- Some or moderate work-related communication necessary among group members
- Manager makes the decisions with input from the team members

This model works best when the manager or the organization needs input to make a decision and when the manager wants to develop team members so that one day they will be able to communicate more effectively with one another and/or be more involved in the decision-making process.

The Participative Team

When a team has reached the participative level, the true definition of a team becomes apparent.

Characteristics of the Participative Team

• Managers have completely developed their team-leadership skills and have also developed the technical and team/interpersonal skills of their team members sufficiently to have the latter be a partner in decision making. This can take many months to do.

• The manager, though still known to everyone on the team and outside of the team as the leader, has no more power in decision making than any team member.

• Team members and the manager need constant communication among each other in order to get the work done. This process can be very time-consuming.

• Team members "own" the product or service and are very concerned with coming up with the best product or service. Their motivation is high.

The Autonomous Team

This kind of team functions very well on its own with some occasional guidance, direction, and boundaries from the manager.

Characteristics of the Autonomous Team

• Members' subject matter expertise and motivation are high.

• Communication is constant among team members. Team members are totally interdependent.

• The manager does not have to be involved in the day-to-day functioning of the team, nor must he or she be present at most team meetings.

• The team enjoys its work and working with one another.

• It takes great effort to get a team to this level, and the benefits to everyone are enormous. However, not every team can become an autonomous team. The team members may not be able to acquire the necessary level of technical and team skills.

• Team members tend to be more technically proficient in many areas than the manager. They are expected to make decisions on their own. These decisions affect the work of the team and/or organization. They are allowed to make many decisions without the manager's prior approval. This does not mean the manager cannot set boundaries and guidelines on the team's decisions.

• Team members share the leadership during team meetings or the day-to-day work, or they rotate the leadership.

• The manager of the autonomous team is free to do other things because the team basically runs itself. She can work on her own projects, develop other teams, work more closely with individual team members, or take on more assignments from her boss.

Because the title of this book is *The First-Time Manager's Guide to Team Building*, our focus is on how to get a team to the developing level (the beginnings of a team) at the minimum, and ideally to the participative level or beyond. We will not focus on the work group, even though many of the strategies used with the developing, participative, and autonomous teams can be used with the work group. See Table 4-1 for a comparison of the work group and the team, keeping in mind the differences that exist among the developing, participative, and autonomous teams.

TABLE 4-1. A COMPARISON OF THE WORK GROUP AND THE TEAM	
The Work Group	*The Team* *(Developing, Participative, or Autonomous)*
Manager or leader makes most decisions and communication tends to be top-down, one-way	Shared or consensus decision making and much more two-way communication
Each team member is accountable for his or her own work	Individual and team accountability
Individual work assignments	Joint work assignments
Manager gives feedback on how team members are doing	Team members and manager give feedback
Dependent on the manager or leader	Interdependent on other team members
Team/interpersonal skills not too important	Team/interpersonal skills are critical

· 5 ·

Mismanaging Your Teams

There are two dangerous conditions that first-time managers often fall victim to: overmanaging and undermanaging. Let's look at undermanaging first.

Undermanaging

Let's say you have a pretty inexperienced team (both in technical skills and team skills) and you manage them as if they were an autonomous team. This is a major mistake.

Inexperienced team members need much more guidance and direction from their managers or team leaders. Some first-time managers expect their team members to learn everything on their own somehow. There are examples of this being true, but not generally speaking. When you undermanage, you are setting up your team members for failure and frustration. Many managers still blame the team, even when their teams' work assignments or projects do not come out as expected. This is pretty unethical behavior. Let me highlight this with a real example.

I once overheard a first-time manager talking with her boss. The boss had expressed some alarm about how one of the manager's projects was going. The first-time manager replied, "I know, I am well aware of it. I cannot believe the team I have. They do not seem to know what they are doing. I suggest you speak directly to them. After all, I cannot be blamed for their mistakes."

Overmanaging

Now, let's turn our attention to the other half of mismanaging teams—overmanaging. Here you have a participative or autonomous team in every sense of the word, and the manager or team leader is acting as if it were a developing team or a work group. She makes the mistake of closely supervising and monitoring the team members when they do not need it. Overmanaging gets teams angry; as a result, they'll do anything to get you off their backs, or, because they are so annoyed, they may undermine your efforts. They do not need all of this attention. This is a classic case of micromanaging.

Micromanaging has gotten a bad rap over the years. There is absolutely nothing wrong with micromanaging if you use it for teams that need close supervision. But there is everything wrong with it when it is used with teams that do not need to be told what to do or to be monitored closely.

Finding Balance

It is crucial that you determine which model best suits your team and that you try to provide the best management approach. When you do this, you have a management match. Matches lead to high morale and high productivity. Overmanaging and undermanaging cause many conflicts between managers and their teams and have led to the downfall of many first-time mangers. They are also two of the biggest reasons teams fail.

You may find the following point interesting and perhaps somewhat insightful when you are considering which team model to employ. When I ask my seminar groups to describe their real-world or fantasy best-team experiences, 98 percent of the time their answers relate to participative or autonomous team experiences. This may motivate you to do whatever you possibly can to get your teams to this high-performing level. Please keep in mind though that not every team can achieve the highest levels of performance, even if you and your organization encourage it. Many team members may not be able to develop the required technical or team skills.

6

Creating a Team-Based Work Environment

Many organizations have realized the great benefits that teams can bring. And hopefully they also realize that it takes great effort to develop a group of individuals into a team that performs at a high level. A team-based organization is one in which much of the work gets done with and through those teams.

There are five conditions organizations should look at or consider before they determine whether they can create a team-based environment. Individual managers can also look at these conditions to see if they can transform their work groups into teams.

The more of these five conditions that are in place the better chance organizations and managers will have in developing team-based organizations and high-performing teams. If any of the conditions are missing, it will be more challenging. Organizations and managers need to assess which of the conditions are missing and then develop strategies to make sure they are in place. I have never really seen a team-based environment or a high-performing team that did not have all of these conditions for transformation in place.

Condition 1. Managerial-Style Paradigm

Managers in an organization have to be behind their teams, support them, and want them to succeed. They have to be willing to engage in two-way communication and allow their teams to be involved in the decision-making process. They cannot be threatened by the team structure, and they cannot fear that their teams can or will know more than they do.

Condition 2. Team Skills

In addition to having the technical skills to perform their jobs, team members also need to be trained to work together as a team. Only when teams learn how to work on their own without close supervision from their managers or team leaders will a team-based organization "happen," and only then will teams reach high levels of performance.

Condition 3. Empowered Team Members

Teams will not succeed or not form at all unless the team members really want to be members of teams. They must want or expect to engage in open communication with their fellow team members and managers and be actively involved in determining what is best for their teams. Many individuals would rather just come to work, do what they are told, and leave. And that is fine as long as they do what they are supposed to. However, for teams to thrive, the team members themselves have to want to be empowered. It helps if the organization and the managers encourage this empowerment and talk to the team members about the importance of their involvement in discussions and decision making.

Condition 4. An Open Approach to Change and Risk

Installing teams and creating a team environment, if it has never been done before, can be a risky proposition. There is no guarantee that teams will work out. Because this is the reality, organizations and their managers have to be open to taking some risks. Change is a risk. And going from work groups to teams is a very big change. If all of the other conditions for transformation are in place, then the risk is much lower.

Because of their cultures, different organizations have different views of risk. Type X organizations are open to change, demand it, and expect it. Type Y organizations are very careful, sometimes too careful, before they engage in change or risk taking. By the time they decide to make a change, they may have lost a big opportunity. Type Z organizations do not change or take any risks unless they are forced to. A team-based organization or high-performing teams have the best chances of succeeding in the Type X and maybe Y organizational cultures.

Condition 5. Human Resources Systems

If you want to get individuals and managers to buy in to the team concept, change your HR systems. For example, if you only rate team members and managers for their individual contributions, you will not really get them to buy in to teamwork. But if you also rate them, promote them, and pay them based on their team contributions or their team-leadership behaviors, then they will take the team concept very seriously.

I also encourage organizations to develop a 360-degree feedback approach. Here, not only does the boss evaluate a manager, but her peers, team members, and, if she has any, customers evaluate her work. She gets a true picture of how she is performing, and she knows that she has to work cooperatively and effectively with everyone. The 360-degree feedback systems are a vital ingredient for team-based organizations.

Closing Up

In this first part of the book we described the high-performing team, discussed the three factors of team life, and reviewed the different team models. Now you should be able to determine which model represents your team today and which model you ultimately want to get your team to. We also pointed out the perils of overmanaging and under managing, and we described the conditions necessary for creating a team-based organization or a high-performing team.

In Part 2, we look at what it takes to make the transition from a staff, team member, or individual contributor role to that of a manager who is building teams. We also look at the barriers you may encounter on the way.

PART TWO

Traveling the Road from Team Member to Manager/Leader of Teams

7

A New Set of Skills

In order to succeed at building teams as a first-time manager, you need a variety of skills. Many of these skills are probably new to you. Developing them will enable you to build a team that may begin at the developing level but eventually, and hopefully, goes to the participative or autonomous level. The benefits of getting your teams to the participative or autonomous levels are enormous for any organization. The members of these high-performing teams produce high-quality work in large quantities and in a quick manner (the three Qs of performance). They also want to keep learning and increasing their skills; they have a higher sense of loyalty to their jobs, their customers, and to the organization; they are the most dependable; and they make smart decisions on how to improve their products or services.

A Combination of Primary Skills and Leadership Skills

As a manager or leader of teams, your major goal is to build high-performing teams that have team spirit (clearly defined roles and responsibilities, open and honest communication, a supportive/knowledgeable manager, decision-making authority, and rewards and recognition). In order to achieve this goal, you will need to demonstrate two major different sets of skills. The first set is called primary skills. These skills include:

• *Planning.* This skill involves determining what the team needs to do in order to reach its goals and the goals of the department or organization. In order to plan, you will need to become as knowledgeable as possible about the work of your team and the technical skills that it needs to do the job. You will have to also plan how your team can develop its team skills and how it will become a high-performing team, if that is your goal.

• *Organizing.* This skill involves focusing on the work of the team and determining who takes on the different roles and responsibilities in order to accomplish the team's goals. Organizing also entails determining how the team members need to work together in order to accomplish these goals; obtaining the resources the team needs; and coordinating its work efforts with other teams, departments, or individuals within the organization.

• *Developing.* This skill involves teaching or getting someone else to teach the technical and team skills the team members need to reach a level of high performance. You also need to develop your team-leadership skills so you can manage the team effectively.

• *Monitoring.* This skill requires checking in on a regular basis to make sure the team's work gets completed. The amount of checking depends on the complexity of the work and the skill level of the team member or team. Monitoring also involves noticing how team members are working with one another (i.e., looking for conflicts, lack of cooperation, etc.) and getting feedback about the team from people outside the team.

• *Evaluating.* This skill involves measuring whether and how well the team met its goals and what it may need to do differently in the future. You need to set up clear, objective ways to measure results. It is always best when the team knows how to do its own measurements. Peter Drucker, the father of modern management, once said that management is measurement.

The second set of skills are leadership behaviors. These are behaviors that, when managers and team leaders get great at them, make people *want* to do what they are supposed to do instead of feel like they *have* to do what they are supposed to. The leadership behaviors provide the right type of environment for the team to succeed. They include:

- Encouraging and motivating the team members
- Actively listening
- Explaining to the team how its job is important and how its job is aligned with the overall mission of the organization
- Staying open-minded and straightforward regarding criticism
- Being persistent
- Maintaining high ethical standards and practices and being a role model for those behaviors
- Getting the team the resources it needs
- Running interference so the team can more readily achieve its goals
- Building trusting relationships through the appropriate use of feedback and self-disclosure (sharing your thoughts and opinions and mistakes with your team)
- Creating a fun, positive work environment where the team's successes are celebrated and recognized

The First-Time Managerial Olympics

The leadership skills are not all that different from the ones my seminar groups listed when describing their best team experiences. Generally speaking, when team members think of their best teams, it seems that the majority remember behaviors associated with leadership skills more than primary skills. But I want to emphasize that both sets of skills are very important. Some first-time managers seem to be better at the primary skills and others excel at the leadership ones. It is a good idea to know where your strengths and gaps are.

Now here's an idea who's time has come. Imagine that coming soon, there is going to be a first-time-manager team-building Olympics. Think of the events as tests of specific primary or leadership skills. Which events would you enter? Which do you think you would win a gold medal in? Which would you never ever think of entering? Answering these questions will give you a good sense of what skill areas you will need to focus on.

Key Points for Team Builders

There are a few key points I need for you to remember and put into practice when building your teams.

Point #1

Your role as an excellent builder of teams is to be willing and able to use a combination both of the primary and leadership skills. The *willing* part of this point means having the motivation or confidence to do it, and the *able* part means having the skills to do it. There is a great difference between these two words.

Point #2

Being a great builder of teams means being able to use the primary and leadership skills. It also means being able to use the right amount of each depending on the needs of your team members. If, for example, your team is at the developing level, you need to have strong primary and leadership skills. You are in charge. When the team moves into the performing level, share these skills, and when a team reaches the autonomous level, the team takes on the responsibility for most of these behaviors. Here is another reason for trying to get your teams to the higher levels of team performance: Your teams will be more in charge of their day-to-day functioning and you will be freed up to focus on other responsibilities.

Point # 3

When a team seems to be discouraged or overwhelmed or there are apparent relationship problems among team members, no matter the level that the team is at, you definitely need leadership skills.

Point # 4

When team members get confused over roles or responsibilities, or the quality of the work is in jeopardy, primary skills become the focus.

Point # 5

Some first-time managers value either the primary or the leadership skills more and tend to use the ones that they value more. This is usually because they are more comfortable with one set of skills over the other. You need to be willing and able to use both.

· 8 ·

Roadblocks on Your Way

There are many reasons why first-time managers do not succeed as team builders. And if they do not succeed, their teams do not succeed either, and vice versa.

Some of the more obvious reasons teams fail are a lack of clear goals, having the wrong people on the team, a lack of resources, poor use or no use of the primary and leadership skills by the team manager, lack of training for team members, work overload, absence of reward and accountability systems, meaningless or boring work projects or assignments, or unrealistic deadlines. Most of these can be attributed to the manager herself, the organization, or a combination of both.

I would now like to discuss what I believe are the biggest barriers to success in your team-building role. Watch out for them! They are you, the first-time manager; mixed messages about the importance of teams; and punishing high-performing teams.

You, the First-Time Manager

Let's look at how first-time managers are a barrier to their own success and their teams' success. Let's be honest and look at the reality of what is going on. Many first-time managers do not really want to be in a managerial or team-building role. They sometimes are "forced" to do so if they want to advance in their organizations or if there is no one else to take on the role, or, for a very practical reason, to earn higher salaries and reap more benefits.

Many people who have been highly successful as individual contributors do not necessarily do well in managerial and team-building roles. Building a team takes a very different set of skills from those needed to perform one's job well as an individual contributor. As an individual contributor your focus was on tasks; now you have to focus on people as well. You were focused on the details of getting your job done, now you have to be much more big-picture-oriented and concerned about what is happening in your department and organization. As an individual contributor you solved problems. Now you will have to define problems for others to solve.

Here is the advice I have for first-time managers if they are the barriers to their own success: You have to develop and feel very comfortable with the skills it takes to be a team leader or builder of teams. You have to really want to be in the business of developing others and you must concentrate less on your own subject-matter expertise. In fact, if you succeed as a manager and team builder, after a period of time you will no longer be as technically proficient in your area of expertise. Your team members will know more than you.

Once you put your mind to team building, you will find it incredibly rewarding and you will most likely be viewed by others as a great asset. Or, to be brutally truthful, if it is something you really do not want to do, consider not taking on or continuing in this role—seriously. You will not be happy and your teams will not grow into high-performing ones. Additionally, you are not really helping out your organization in the long run.

Another managerial barrier is the desire to retain the power or control for oneself and not share it with others. Many first-time managers, and experienced ones as well, like their teams to know that they are in charge. They do not allow their teams to develop into high-performing ones. They want to make the decisions and call all the shots. This desire to control may be due to some managers' perceptions that their teams cannot work well without their close supervision. Often these perceptions are inaccurate. We tend to see or believe what we want to.

Other managers may believe that they are the only ones who know what decision to make, but let's face it: with some training, education, and guidance the majority of teams will be able to make their own decisions if allowed to.

Other first-time managers have not developed flexibility yet. They tend to use the managerial style that they are most comfortable with. Sometimes this works out, sometimes it doesn't. For example, a first-time manager may be the hands-off type who likes his team to work on its own, make its own decisions, etc. This sounds pretty good to me. But what if the team is not able to do that? The manager has to change his style, get out of his comfort zone, and be more hands-on. This is where the flexibility comes in. The manager should always adapt to the needs of his team rather than expect the team to adapt to his managerial or team leadership style.

As a first-time developer of high-performing teams, you need to truly want your teams to perform at their highest levels possible considering your teams' limitations and organizational constraints. You never want to be a barrier to your teams' development. I promise you that getting your teams to develop and succeed can be one of your biggest accomplishments and biggest joys.

Mixed Messages About the Importance of Teams

Many organizations and their managers preach teamwork. They talk about the importance of teams at company-wide meetings. Their newsletters and other publications have articles on the importance of teamwork. When you walk through the corridors and factory floors, one sees posters of teams (usually athletic depictions) plastered throughout. And their company visions, mission statements, or guiding principles emphasize teamwork as well.

But more often than not, the reality is that many companies and their managers do not reward teamwork or hold people accountable for not working well on teams. They only emphasize or reognize the team member's individual contribution. When organizations and managers do this, they are sending a mixed message.

At one of my first jobs years ago, I got one of these mixed messages regarding teamwork. I was working in the organizational-development-and-change department of a Fortune 500 company in New York City. I was in charge of developing and conducting organizational surveys. The company's big theme at the time was "we are one big team." That message was spread in every conceivable way. I believe to this day they were trying to brainwash us into believing that teams were what the company was after.

But when I (and everyone else in the company) got a performance appraisal or when I got a salary adjustment or when I was being considered for a promotion, the word *team* was never mentioned. I was rated, salaried, reviewed, etc. solely on my individual contributions. I soon got the message that this team stuff was just lip service. I hate to admit it now, but I learned to pretend to be a good team player yet watched out only for me.

Mixed messages are confusing and definitely affect morale and productivity. They counteract the efforts that the team manager and the team members put into building their teams.

I strongly believe that it is only when organizations and managers reward, recognize, and hold people accountable for their team *and* their individual contributions that a team environment will truly develop. The message about teams has to hit the pocketbook. Only when people get the message that they will be evaluated on their team contributions will they work on becoming great team players. The same would be true for team leaders and managers who are builders of teams. They too need to be evaluated on how well they build their teams and not just told that teams are important or that there is a team environment.

Punishing High-Performing Teams

You would think that as team builders we would want to reward our high-performing teams and not punish them. But I have noticed far too often that managers, team leaders, or organizations often punish their best teams for being so great. When we or our organizations do this, we cause the team to fail. Let's look at the case of Sheila V., a first-time manager of teams, to illustrate my point.

The Sheila V. Case

Sheila is a first-time manager at an engineering company in northern California. She has been managing three different teams for the last year. I have been working with Sheila, explaining the importance of not punishing teams for being great. Sheila recently told me how, inadvertently, she was punishing her participative team and now she knows why its work has begun to slip. She had just come to realize that she was doing this. Her two other teams are at the developing level.

Sheila said that when the participative team would finish projects ahead of schedule, she would give it some tasks that the other two teams did not finish. Other times, when she was too busy to do some of her own work (and really did not want to do it), she would divide it up among the team members. She knew they would just do it and not complain about it. This was a form of punishment.

Sheila also told me that several months ago the team was invited to present its research at a national professional conference. She made the team decline the invitation because she did not want to lose them for an entire week. Who would do all the work around the office? This was a form of punishment.

Sheila gave me one last example of how she was punishing her really good team members. She said she would pair her more-experienced team members up with her less-experienced team members from her two developing teams. They were not doing well technically and she wanted the more-experienced people to coach them. Sometimes she would even get requests from other departments for this type of assistance and willingly obliged their requests. What Sheila forgot was that even though there was an obvious benefit to the less-skilled team members, the more-skilled ones would have rather been doing their own assignments or learning something new themselves! This was also a form of punishment.

I am glad to say that Sheila has seen the error of her ways and no longer punishes her high-performing team members. If we keep punishing our teams for being so good, eventually they will stop being so good. We need to reward them and give them new growth opportunities so they will remain at a high level of performance.

• 9 •

Getting to the New Road

Most life changes take us through three phases: stopping, stalling, and starting over—the three S's of change. When we transition from individual contributors to team leaders or first-time managers, we go through the same three phrases of change. We will know that a change has been a triumph if we reach and feel comfortable at the third phase. If we do not reach the third phase of change, the change will not be a success. If a first-time manager does not reach this phase, he will not thrive as a team builder, or in a broader sense, a first-time manager.

Stopping

The first S or phase is called stopping. Here, we stop what we are currently doing. For example, if you are making the transition from team member to the manager of that team, you stop being the technician or the team member, and you need to stop identifying with the group that you used to be a member of. You have to stop talking, if you ever have, about management or the organization in a negative way and be a strong supporter of organizational change if you were not one before.

Stalling

The second phase or S in the change process is called stalling. In the stalling phase things seem chaotic, confusing, and you are uncertain how things will turn out. You will probably have the urge to go back to the way things were. For example, as a first-time manager you may not know the best way to communicate with your team, whom to ask for advice, what to do when team members are not cooperative, or even which team model to use. Stalling is very normal and it is important to go through this phase. Try not to resist it. The danger with the stalling phase is that if you remain in it too long, you do not get to the last phase or S, starting over.

Starting Over

In this last phase you begin to learn what is required of you, begin to develop your new skills, and become comfortable with your new role. This phase can take a long time, so prepare for it. Do not get upset if you do not become a great team builder overnight.

When I am working with new team builders or first-time managers, I often ask them two questions to get them to think about how they can eventually get to the third S. The questions are: What do you have to stop doing right now so you can succeed in your new role? What do you have to begin doing so you can succeed in your new role? Try answering these questions and you will be well on your way to building high-performing teams and succeeding in your new role.

The 10 Steps of Team Building

You have now moved into your new role as the manager/leader/ builder of a team or are about to. You are either in the starting phase or the stalling one. What do you do now? How do you get started on building your team? Here's the answer in 10 easy steps. That is, the steps are very easy to understand, but a bit more diffi- cult to implement.

You must do each step. Never skip a step. And I am making one assumption with these 10 steps: that you are beginning from scratch and building a new team. But the reality could be that you are inheriting an existing team. Even if the latter is true, you should follow or review many of the same steps.

When building your team, you should use the same 10 steps whether you are a first-time manager or a more-experienced one and whether your team members are new to working on teams or are more experienced. The only difference is that you will probably move through the steps faster if you or your team members are experienced with teams.

Do the first four steps on your own before even meeting with your team. You want to have your own thoughts and action plans set before you have your first team meetings. Just because you are doing these steps on your own does not mean that you cannot get help from your manager, your mentor, other managers, or experienced team leaders.

Step 1: Getting Upper-Management Support

Upper-management support can make or break how you succeed in building your team. You need to know that your immediate manager and upper management supports your efforts to develop your team according to the team model you believe would best serve the interests of the organization. You also need support in developing your leadership skills and your team's technical and team skills. You need to ascertain whether the organization will assist in this development or whether you can go to an external source. And upper management needs to support you by providing you and your team with the resources needed for your team's success. Lack of upper-management support for team-building efforts is one of the biggest reasons teams do not succeed.

In order to obtain and maintain upper management's support, you need to demonstrate how the team's goals and work align with the goals of the organization. You also need to show in very tangible and measurable terms how well your team is doing. If you get the results upper management is looking for, you will get more and more autonomy to manage your own team, even if the organization is fairly directive in its management approach.

It is also important for you and your management or manager to agree that you will be the focal point for your team, not them. It is dangerous, for example, when management goes directly to your team and gives it directives without your knowledge or undermines your decisions. When this occurs, your team members will stop going to you when they have issues or concerns and will go directly to your boss or your management. It will be confusing for them and outright disastrous for you. Both the team members and management will view you as someone who cannot make decisions and someone who is not really in charge. If management does not reach out to you to discuss how you both will work together in building your team, then it is your obligation to approach them.

Step 2: Define the Purpose of Your Team

You need to think about why your team was formed or why it currently exists. What is it there to accomplish? What are its specific or ongoing goals? Even before you meet with your team, you need to have the answers to these questions. Does the team exist to solve a problem, come up with a new approach, or improve an existing process? If you are not clear on its purpose, the team members will definitely not be. You might need to clarify how management sees the purpose of the team to make sure you both see it the same way. Then you will be able communicate this to your team.

Many first-time managers believe that if the purpose of the team is clear to them then it is also clear to the team members. This is not necessarily true. Once you know exactly what the purpose is, you need to communicate it to your team members at the first team meeting.

Step 3: Identify Time Frames

In this step you identify the project due date or when the work needs to get completed. You also identify specific milestones; that is, what actions need to happen by what dates. These two statements apply more to a project team. But you will probably also need to develop certain time frames for ongoing teams and individual team members.

Step 4: Select the Team Members

If we are talking about an ongoing or existing team, then your team members have already been selected and you are taking over from a previous manager or team leader. However, if you are putting together a project team for a specific purpose, adding members to an existing team, or forming a new team, you need to identify what skills, experience, and knowledge will best accomplish the team's goals.

One caution if this is a project team. We always try to find the best people for our project teams. But if we only use the best people, we are creating two major organizational problems. First, we are not developing other staff members. We need all staff to be developed if we want our organizations to succeed. Second, we may be overloading the best staff members, and if we keep doing that, eventually they will burn out or leave. Thus, it is a good policy, if you can work it out administratively or politically, to use volunteers for your project teams. They tend to be more committed to the project because they have a strong interest in being on it.

Core, Extended, and External Team Members. Your team members, whether they are selected or are volunteers, are what we call core team members. Extended team members are individuals within the organization who can be resources or subject-matter experts for your core team. For example, if one of your core members needs assistance, information, or advice, she will know who in the organization, besides the core team members, she can count on. You or the organization identifies the extended team members and notifies them in advance that they are extended members. Once again, it is good to get your extended members to volunteer.

External team members are individuals outside the organization who also act as resources for your core team members. They can be professional associations, colleagues from other organizations, or known experts in their fields. From time to time your core team members may have to rely on these extended team members because no one within the organization is of assistance to them. These extended team members are either identified at the beginning of a project or during it, depending on when the need arises.

How to Find the Best New Team Members Possible. If you have to hire one or more team members, find the best ones possible. Let's review what it takes to do that.

The first consideration is where to find the team member. The usual avenues are recruiting companies, headhunters, advertisements, college recruiting, job fairs, or personal references. I believe that personal references are the best. Many organizations give the referring employee a bounty or a monetary fee for finding a candidate who is hired. If the new team member does not work out, then the organization takes the fee back. Even though I just said personal referrals are the most effective way to recruit new team members, the organization must make every effort to recruit from the larger community.

Next, screen the application or resume to determine if the potential team member's background matches the requirements for the job. You should know exactly what the job requirements are before beginning the screening. Many people know how to prepare excellent resumes and can easily write ones that contain the buzz or key words and list the skills that the position calls for. Therefore, determining the best team member just from a resume is quite challenging and not all that accurate.

When reviewing a resume, look for things that may need clarification during the phone screening. Examples include overlapping job dates; long gaps between jobs; not enough information; poor grammar and spelling; a mismatch between the applicant's description of his or her skills and those required by the job; extensive training, certifications, or advanced degrees despite a relatively low position within the applicant's current organization; or listing "personal reasons" to explain why the applicant left previous jobs.

A great skill to have when reviewing resumes is to be able to read between the lines. I once reviewed a resume that said the applicant left previous positions because he and his bosses were never able to agree on important decisions. I read between the lines and felt that the applicant was an individual who probably wanted it his way. He did have great skills and an excellent educational background, so I interviewed him anyway.

I justified my suspicion during the telephone interview. He was not a team player, and that was a major requirement for the job. I found out why during the interview. He felt that because of his educational background he knew best and believed that his team members should defer to his knowledge and experience.

If a potential team member passes the telephone interview, then you can invite her in for a formal face-to-face interview. Prepare many questions in advance. The goal of the interview is to find out as much about the potential team member as you possibly can. These questions should seek information about the individual's skills, knowledge, and abilities. Try to get applicants to give you lots of work-related examples of how they have used their skills and knowledge on the job. They should do about 75 percent of the talking.

Keep your questions open-ended and let the interviewee answer at length. For example, you might say, "Please give me some examples of what you have done in order to remain knowledgeable about your competitive environment. Include what you learned about your competitors, products, services, and technology trends." Questions about the applicant's work attitude, work style, interest in coming to work for your organization, decision-making style, temperament, or ability to be a team player are equally important. For example, if you are trying to find out about a candidate's resourcefulness, ask, "What are some examples of circumstances in which you were expected to do certain activities and went beyond the call of duty?" If there is not a good fit, the person, even though he or she may have the right skills, may not work out.

When you are interviewing someone who has no prior work experience, such as a recent graduate, you may have to ask mostly hypothetical questions about specific job-related situations. For example, you might ask, "What would you do if a team member did not share information that you needed to complete your part of a project?"

Be careful with your questions. There are many that are inappropriate or even illegal. For example, you cannot ask anything about the applicant's age, physical appearance, marital status, parental status, native languages, disabilities, what clubs or organizations the applicant may belong to, the applicant's personal finances, or hobbies or activities outside of work. In fact, I highly suggest that you only ask questions that are directly related to job performance. If you cannot connect your question to the requirements of the job, do not ask it! There have been countless instances of job candidates suing companies for improper questioning during interviews.

Have a format for conducting your interview so each potential team member has a similar interviewing experience and a fair chance of succeeding. First, greet the candidate and establish rapport by asking questions such as, "How was your trip here?" or "What do you think of the weather we have been having lately?" Then tell the candidate what is going to happen during the interview process and about how long it is going to take. Next, engage the candidate in the question-and-answer period, which should be the bulk of the interview. Tell him a bit about the organization, answer his questions, and tell him what the next steps in the interview process are. You want to conduct a very professional interview. Even if the interviewee is not the one you select to join your team, you still want that person walking away from the interview feeling like this is a great company to work for.

The final two parts of the interview process include determining which potential team members best fit the position and then telling each of them whether they were offered the position. Some first-time managers wait too long before they get back to the interviewees. During this interim, an excellent candidate may have found another position.

Teams at the participative and autonomous levels can help you choose the best new team member for the job. I encourage you to let your team members interview the candidates and spend time with them. Some companies in which I have consulted invite the candidate in for an entire day or two (and often compensate them for their time). This allows everyone to meet and to get to know the potential team member. You can even have the candidate work on regular assignments or projects. After those couple of days, you will have a really good sense of whether that person has the tangible and intangible skills you are looking for.

One-on-Ones. Some first-time managers like to meet one-on-one with each team member in order to get to know them before having the initial team meetings. I think that is a very good idea and most always facilitates a relationship between the manager and her team members. At these one-on-ones try not to go into the same details that you will cover in your initial team meetings. It's redundant.

One-on-ones during team formation or when you are taking over a team are designed for you to get to know your team members on a personal basis, and vice versa. These initial one-on-ones can also address some issues that particular team members have with you, the team, or the project. For instance, a team member might resent you becoming the manager or project leader, because he wanted the job. Or another team member may have some issues with the work the team does or is about to do or with some of the other team members. You can also pick up some very valuable information about organizational procedures, culture, and politics during your one-on-ones, especially if you are new to the organization or your managerial role.

I highly encourage you to continue having one-on-ones throughout the team member's tenure, even if you are lucky enough to get the team member to the highest performance level possible. One-on-ones reinforce the goals of the team, allow you to be proactive in solving problems or concerns, and cement your working relationships. It is good to follow a particular format when conducting your one-on-ones. You can use this format to conduct performance and development discussions with the entire team as well.

Begin the discussion by asking the team member what he felt was excellent about his performance or progress since your last performance and development discussion. Then you share your views. Then ask the team member how he can continue developing, progressing, and building upon his current strengths. Then you give your thoughts on that. Then ask the team member if there is anything he is not satisfied with regarding his performance and development. And you give your opinions next. When there are any differences of opinion between yourself and the team member, this is the time to discuss them. You will need very tangible examples to prove your points. Obviously, you will have much fewer, if any, disconnects if you conduct regularly scheduled performance and development discussions.

Steps 5-10, Meeting with the Team

Once you have done your initial planning work in steps 1-4, you can get together with all of your team members at the same time and talk about all of the basic elements of how the team members and you will function together. The first few meetings are vital for establishing an effective working relationship. The remaining steps take place at these first few meetings. Here are my recommendations for what you should accomplish at these meetings.

Step 5: Team-Member Openings

Have team members introduce themselves if they are not already familiar with one another and get some initial thoughts from them on how they feel being on the team. If it is an existing team, have the team members talk about how the team is doing. If it is a new team, ask the team members about their prior team experiences and what they want this team to be like.

Many team leaders expect that after a period of time working together, the team members will become friends. They feel they have failed their teams if everyone does not befriend one another. Friendships are fine, but friendships do not make a high-performing team. Depth of skills, knowledge, and experience are what ultimately make a high-performing team.

Step 6: Share the Overall Purpose

Talk about why the team was formed, its overall purpose or goal, and how the overall purpose ties into the mission of the department or organization. Clear up any misconceptions the team members have about the purpose of the team or why it was formed. If it is an existing team, confirm that the members all agree on the purpose of the team.

Step 7: Team Name

If it is feasible to do so in your organization, have the team members name the newly formed team. If it is an existing team without a name, have the team members create one. The name should reflect the purpose or work of the team. It is always best if the team members name the team on their own without your assistance. If they cannot, help them out. Of course you may have to give them certain parameters about what is and is not acceptable. This is a great way to begin your involvement with your team. They immediately see that you are letting them make a decision. A team name also gives the members a sense of identity, and it is one of the first ways you get team members to bond.

If you can, keep away from team names that prevent others in the organization from understanding what the team does. Some teams go too far into orbit and come up with names that are very innovative or creative but not practical for the organizational environment or culture. I once worked in an organization where one of the teams was named Route 66. The company manufactured flatware and glassware. I could not imagine what Route 66 had to do with these products. So I asked. I was told that the team just liked the name, so they decided to use it.

The team's name basically needs to identify what the team does.

At this stage, the name does not have to be written in stone. Give the team a chance to live with it for a few weeks and always leave the option open for changing it.

Step 8: Create the Team Mission Statement and Goals

A mission statement is a written statement that identifies the purpose of the team or its reason for being. A mission statement is usually one or two sentences, and it does not describe how the team will accomplish its purpose, just what its purpose is. Here is an example: "The Gamma team sets up protocols to test for the efficacy of all experimental drugs manufactured by XYZ Corporation."

The team mission statement should also reflect or align itself with the overall mission of the organization. Many high-performing teams include a mission statement in all of their published documents or literature and/or post it in their work areas for all to see and as a reminder to themselves.

Just as with the team name, team members should try to come up with the mission statement on their own. This empowers them, gives them a sense of pride, and is one of their first accomplishments as a team.

Another very strong reason to have a team mission is to keep your team on track. You will sometimes run into teams or individual team members who focus on work that has little to do with the mission of the team. When this occurs, ask them how what they are currently working on connects to the team's mission. This is a very easy and nonconfrontational way to get them back on track.

Once the team mission statement is written, you need to set goals for each team member. The goals should align with the team mission statement. Your team members must know how their goals also serve the greater purpose of the organization. When establishing goals, it is best to ask the team members to come up with what they believe their goals are, review them, and come to an agreement on what their goals actually are. It is also possible to set goals for the overall team and then let the team figure out what each team member needs to do to achieve these goals. I recommend that in the early stages of team development you do not do this. It is better for you to help each team member establish his or her own set of goals. When a team reaches the higher levels of performance, it will be able to set team goals.

When writing goals for each team member, it is best to follow the well-known SMART method. The acronym states that all goals should be specific, measurable, achievable, relevant, and time framed.

Make sure the goals are very specific so the team member knows exactly what she has to do. It is also best to have clear ways to measure whether the goal has been achieved. It is even better if a team member herself can measure how she is doing.

When setting goals, it is a good idea to make sure the team member can actually achieve the goal. You may want to stretch the team members a bit so they can achieve more than they initially thought they could. But, if the goal is unrealistic or too difficult to achieve, you are setting up the team members for failure and frustration.

Goals should also be relevant, and as we said, tie in to the mission statement of the team and the mission of the entire organization. Every single team member should be able to tell you or anyone else how his or her goal is relevant to what the organization does.

Finally, every goal should have a time frame to it so it can eventually be measured. Time frames can vary and be ongoing or definite. For example, a time frame may be every day or every month or by the end of the year.

Things change on teams, in departments, and in organizations. That means you have to review and revise each team member's goals in a timely manner. You never want a team member working on a goal that is no longer practical or needed. Also, as mentioned previously, you want both a team's and team members' performance appraisals to reflect how well they achieved their goals.

Step 9: Core Team Issues

Discussing core team issues will be your first demonstration of how well you can facilitate discussions. You are making a first impression here, so it is very important that you succeed. If you do, you are off to a great start with your team. This is why you must be very prepared before entering step 9 because it contains much information vital to the functioning of the team.

The time devoted to bringing up and discussing core team issues depends on the complexities of the team's goals, the relationships the team members have with one another, and their skill levels, both technical and team. If you can arrange it, having a one- or two-day off-site for this step and perhaps all of the other team-building steps would be a wise move on your part. Not only will you and the team be able to focus exclusively on these steps, but you will be well on your way toward developing a team camaraderie and cohesiveness.

The following items are usually discussed at this time:

- The specific activities and time frames that you will hold the team accountable for

- Your philosophy on teams and the importance of this team's mission

- How you plan on managing the team now, and your vision of how your management approach will change in the future

- How and why you want the team members to work with one another now and in the future

- Each team member's specific roles and responsibilities and the specific procedures each person must follow to accomplish his or her work

- How the team now or in the future will be interdependent and how that will work

- The resources available to the team—equipment, supplies, and people (core, extended, and external)

- Logistics—where and when the team will meet and any re
  sponsibilities team members may have in these meetings
- Training schedule—how you or others will work with the
  team members to develop both their technical and team skills
- Explanations of what is meant by team skills and why they
  are so important (and this is the time to begin doing some
  team-building exercises)
- Discussions about how the organization will reward the team
  for its accomplishments and how it will hold the team accountable for achieving results
- Any concerns, questions, etc. that the team has at this time

Step 10: Establishing Team Norms

The last step in the start-up process of team development and team
building is having the team, preferably on its own but with some
guidance from you if needed, establish guiding principles, ground
rules, or team norms (all these terms are synonyms). Team norms
describe how the team members will interact and behave with one
another, especially at team meetings. A big mistake many first-
time managers make is deciding on their own what these team
norms will be and imposing them on their teams. If teams create
them on their own, they are much more likely to stick to them. You
have given them the ownership.

My preference is to have teams create their norms at this time
in the team-building process. Others recommend that you create
them closer to step five or six of the 10-step process. I am sure it
can work either way. I prefer doing it at this time because I like
to give the team members the opportunity to view each other's
behaviors and get to know each other a bit better. When this occurs, they will better be able to come up with the group norms that
they want to abide by.

Team norms vary from team to team. They are usually based on
the nature of the team's work, the level of the team's development,
and the personalities of the team members. Some of the more tradi-

tional or typical team norms include respecting different points of view, allowing everyone to participate in discussions, having one person speak at a time, restricting side conversations, helping each other out, putting the team before any individual concerns, starting and ending meetings on time, sticking to the agenda, being able to voice your opinion when you disagree without any consequence or retribution, or speaking up when certain team member behaviors are problematic for the progress of the team.

Each team member should get a copy of the team norms. The team should review them often. I also recommend posting them on a wall or bulletin board if the team has a regular meeting location.

Team norms are not written in stone. They can be dropped, altered, or new ones can be added. If I had to pick one strategy that, overall, works best for controlling difficult team behaviors and for keeping meetings running smoothly, it is having teams develop norms that they agree to operate by.

Your Job Is Just Beginning

Once you have covered the 10 steps to team building, your job is definitely not over. In fact it is just beginning. The focus of your work now becomes developing your team by giving it the technical and team skills it needs so it can be as self-sufficient and interdependent as possible. Your ongoing teams, compared to your project teams, usually have a much greater amount of time to go through the 10-step process.

Also keep in mind that when a team member leaves or when a new member joins, everything goes back to zero. You and the team have to go through many of the 10 steps again. During and after completing steps 5–10, you need to hold regular team meetings to see how the work is progressing and how team members are getting along. The way you lead your meetings will have a big impact on your relationship with your team members and how well your team develops into a high-performing team.

Now let's look at how to run a successful meeting.

Leading Your Meetings

When your team is at the developing level, you have the responsibility of leading the meeting on your own. You need to decide what the content of the meeting will be and how to pace it as well. When your team's performance improves, you gradually transfer many of the meeting responsibilities to it. And when a team has reached the highest levels of performance, it becomes responsible for leading its own meetings. Often high-performing teams rotate their leadership or the team member who has the most expertise on the meeting topic takes charge.

Your key meeting-leader responsibilities during the time your team is developing include:

• *Determining the Meeting's Purpose.* You need to know in advance why you are having the meeting and want you want to accomplish.

• *Deciding Which Team Members Need to Be at the Meeting.* In the early stages I suggest having all team members present. As the team develops and if the meeting is only to review and/or discuss certain aspects of the work of the team, then only the team members who really need to be there should be present. However, if the meeting is to discuss how the team is doing or progressing or how team members are working interdependently, then all team members must be present.

• *Coordinating Meeting Logistics.* Conduct your meeting in a location where you and the team members will not be disturbed. Make sure all the equipment, if you are using any, works. Do this before the meeting begins. And if you need any supplies or refreshments, make sure they are also there before the meeting begins.

• *Starting Meetings on Time.* You want to send a message that everyone's time is valuable. You never want some team members waiting for other team members. And if you are inviting an extended or external member to your meeting, make sure that person is there on time as well. A big mistake team-meeting leaders make is starting the meeting over when someone who is "important" arrives late. This undermines the trust that team members have in you. It is also very important to end your team meetings on time. Team members have work to do, calls to make, and may have to attend other meetings. It is an expensive proposition having meetings. You are taking your team members away from their regular work. That is costly. Try to have the shortest meetings possible. On the other hand, meetings, especially meetings that address how the team is functioning, are imperative for your team to succeed.

• *Creating a Specific Agenda.* Prepare an agenda in advance and distribute it to all those attending the meeting. Each agenda item should have a time frame assigned to it, and it is important to stick to that time frame. Assign some agenda items to different team members. This will get them more involved in the meeting, and by doing this it becomes your team's meeting as well as yours. You have begun to develop a partnership. If a team member or invited guest brings up a topic that is not related to the agenda, table it. A lot of successful meeting leaders have what is called a parking-lot chart in the room. When somebody wants to discuss something not on the agenda, the topic is written on a post-it note and placed on the parking lot. If there is time at the end of the meeting, the team discusses the topic. If not, it is put on the next meeting's agenda. As your team develops, you can involve it in setting the agenda.

• *Controlling the Meeting Process.* Make sure the meeting is running smoothly. Address any difficult or challenging participant behaviors by referring to the norms you established during the 10 steps of team building. Encourage everyone to participate and create an environment where this can happen. You will have some team members who do not feel comfortable participating at meetings, especially when a team is first developing. I often tell these team members before the meeting to be prepared to talk on a specific topic or that they are expected to give their opinions on one of the agenda items. This almost always works. These team members feel more confident in participating.

As the meeting leader, you may need some help. That is, you may not be able to do everything yourself. You may want a couple of your team members to take on some of the meeting-leadership responsibilities. For example, you could have a timekeeper who would make sure that the meeting is staying on schedule. You could also have a note taker who, at the end of the meeting, reviews the key points and sends this summary to all team members. And when the meeting is over you could have someone lead a discussion on how the meeting went and what the team would do differently next time.

Keep the following seven-step list handy. It will remind you of what you need to think of to have a productive meeting.

1. Is the meeting really necessary? Could I have a virtual meeting or send out the information via e-mail?
2. What are the results I expect to get from the meeting?
3. What topics and issues will we discuss?
4. Have I developed my agenda with time frames and distributed it before the meeting?
5. How will I measure success?

6. What role will I play and what other roles do we need?
7. Who should attend the meeting?

Closing Up

In this part of the book we have looked at what it takes for a first-time manager (and her organization) to move into a team-builder role. The first-time manager has to develop a new set of skills, which include the primary and leadership skills, and know when to use each one. She has to avoid the barriers that often cause teams to fail—her own attitude, sending mixed messages about the importance of teamwork, and punishing high-performing teams. A first-time manager also needs to recognize that any change goes through three classic phases and a change is not successful until one has reached the third phase: starting over.

We reviewed the very important 10 steps of team building and discussed how to run effective team meetings and one-on-ones. We also talked about how to interview potential team members who are new to your team and the organization. Following the steps to team building and incorporating all the other suggestions will surely help you get started in your new role as a builder of teams.

After you have gone through the 10 steps to team building and think your team is ready to grow, you can focus on building team spirit. Once your teams have developed team spirit, they are well on their way to becoming high-performing teams. There are five keys or signs that your team has developed team spirit:

- It has clearly defined roles and responsibilities.
- It has open and honest communication.
- It has a supportive and knowledgeable manager/leader.
- It has decision-making authority.
- It receives rewards and recognitions

In Part 3 of the book we will look at the five keys to developing team spirit and how to incorporate them into your team.

• P A R T T H R E E •

Developing a Team Spirit

Team-Spirit Key #1:
Clear Roles and Responsibilities

Every team member must know exactly what her specific job-related role and responsibilities are and what is expected from her. She should also know the roles, responsibilities, and expectations of every other team member. When all of your team members have gained this knowledge, they are on their way to developing the first key of team spirit. I have witnessed many teams where the team members are not aware of exactly what the other team members do. It is quite difficult to get these teams to a participative or autonomous level. In fact, the lack of any of the five keys to team spirit is a barrier to developing high-performing teams.

The benefit of having clear roles and responsibilities is that team members better understand how the team goals will be achieved and whom to go to when they need help or when a particular job or function is not being achieved or accomplished. Additionally, when each team member clearly knows what her role and responsibilities are, she better understands how her job fits into the bigger picture of what the team, department, and organization are there to accomplish.

Technical Roles

When team members are first learning about one another's roles and responsibilities, it is very useful for each team member to prepare a description of her responsibilities for the team. These descriptions increase each member's understanding of the duties of their colleagues, and it clarifies each member's technical role.

The following five questions are helpful for assembling such an inventory:

1. What are the major jobs and work products for which you are responsible?
2. What jobs or work products do you need to coordinate with other core team members?
3. What aspects of your work are you unclear about? What aspects of others' work are you unclear about?
4. What responsibilities is the team not addressing?
5. Does the team need any other technical expertise that the current team members cannot provide? Are extended and/or external team members needed?

I also suggest creating an electronic technical-skills bank with your team or for your team. In order to do this, team members list all of their current technical skills, their level of expertise in them, any degrees or certifications they have accumulated, special courses they have taken, etc. With a skill bank in place, team members will know whom to contact when they need help or assistance. Actually, a company should have a technical-skills bank that includes every single staff member. Most companies, when they create an online company-wide skills bank, realize that they already have many of the talents that they need in-house and do not have to hire consultants.

Task Roles and Process Roles

In addition to the clearly defined technical or subject-matter expertise roles, team members have to learn and take on other roles in order to develop team spirit. These other roles are called task roles and process roles. Task and process roles are part of team-skill development and are very important roles if team members are to get to a high-performing level.

When a team is in the initial phases of its development, the team leader or manager takes on the responsibility for performing all or most of the task and process roles. But as teams learn to work on their own more and become more interdependent, team members gradually take these roles. The task and process roles may come naturally to some team members, but most will need to be taught what they are, how to use them, and then get feedback on how they are performing them. Learning and becoming comfortable with these roles should be part of all team-building programs. Hopefully, your organization provides this type of team training.

Task Roles

Task roles help the team accomplish its goals. They help get a job done quickly and efficiently. There are five kinds of task roles.

1. *The Initiator.* The initiator helps the team get started. She does this by suggesting or stating assignments, projects, tasks, or goals, and the time frames involved. The initiator also has the group clearly define what its specific roles and responsibilities will be on the task or project, what procedures it needs to follow, and whom it needs to interact with in order to accomplish the work.

2. *The Closer.* The closer helps the team make decisions and reminds people of deadlines. It would not be unusual for someone taking on this role to speak directly to a team member and get him or her to finish the outstanding part of the project or work. This role has a very bottom-line focus.

3. *The Clarifier.* This role clears up any misunderstanding or confusion about the work that the team is performing. The clarifier also offers examples to help the team understand specific points, details, or different opinions on how the team should proceed. Ad-

ditionally, clarifiers help team members who may not be fluent in the team's language or terminology.

4. *The View Searcher.* This person asks the team for its opinions during team meetings and discussions. She also asks for new ideas or innovations to improve any of the current work processes or procedures.

5. *The Subject-Matter Expert (SME).* This person offers facts or additional useful information. The SME makes suggestions on how the team can improve any aspects of its specific products or procedures. The SME may have the knowledge, experience, or skills that none of the other team members possess.

Process Roles

Process roles help a team work more effectively together. These roles help team morale; help team communication; help develop team camaraderie; and provide a fun, motivated environment where all team members can contribute to their fullest. There are four kinds of process roles.

1. *The Communicator.* This person helps the team communicate by encouraging everyone to participate, asking people to speak up if they haven't, facilitating discussion, preventing certain team members from monopolizing the team's time, and being a model for active listening. She reminds the team of its behavioral norms and holds team members to them.

2. *The Process Observer.* During team meetings or discussions this individual(s) observes how the group is functioning as a team and gives her feedback at the end of the meeting or the beginning of the next one. Feedback includes comments on how the team communicated, whether some team members seemed to withdraw, whether the team stuck to its agenda and time frames, whether any team-member behaviors were destructive, and how the team leader, if there was one, did. The following are sample questions the process observer would ask.

- What is the quality of our work interactions?
- Are we giving personal and task-related feedback?
- Are there underlying animosities?
- How open are we with each other?
- What is required for us to trust each other?
- Do we share our perceptions about each other?
- How satisfied are we with each other and our interaction?
- Are there individuals who are not doing their part or are there individuals who are preventing you from doing your part?
- How are we demonstrating our interdependence?
- Do we work together with spirit, excitement, and enthusiasm?

3. *The Motivator/ Supporter.* Teams or individuals will sometimes lose their energy level or enthusiasm when they run into some roadblocks or the project or work becomes more difficult than they initially thought. This is the time when the team needs someone to take on the motivator role. The motivator encourages and inspires the team to keep going, creates a fun environment, gives lots of positive feedback, and puts tense situations into their wider context. This person is also there to support any particular team member who may be having an especially rough time. The motivator acts as a sounding (or venting) board.

4. *The Public Relater.* When I used to manage teams, I was always relieved when one of my team members became great at this role. It really helped the team feel good about what it was doing, and, as with the motivator/supporter role, kept motivation high. Public relaters go around the department or the organization telling everyone how great the team is doing (hopefully it is true!). As a result of the efforts of the public relaters, I would always have individuals from other teams and departments trying to get onto my teams, and upper management would always give my teams the resources they needed.

Role Rotation

Certain team members will naturally gravitate to certain task or process roles. They do this because they have had prior experience with these roles or they have the skill or even the personality to perform them well. This is great if it occurs on your teams. I would suggest, nevertheless, that each team member learn each of these roles in case he or she needs to develop those skills or does not naturally take on certain roles. Many experienced team leaders regularly rotate the different task and process roles among team members, thus guaranteeing that each member is able to perform each role.

I really want to emphasize the importance of team members possessing these task and process skills, which are part of what I call team skills. Many first-time managers focus on what teams or team members know technically. But they also need to focus on how they work together to achieve results. A team can have very skilled and knowledgeable members, but without the task and process skills, it will not likely accomplish its goals on its own.

When you are developing your teams, you should constantly talk about how they are working together and not just how the work itself or the projects are going. Always make this discussion one of the team-meeting agenda items. I often make it the top agenda item when the team is having problems. Teams that reach the participative or autonomous levels generally do their own team analyses. It is part of getting trained in teamwork. But there may be occasions where you have to step in and lead the discussion.

The Manager/Team Leader Role

As I have already said, your major job in team building is to develop your team into a high-performing one, keeping in mind that it may not be possible for all teams to reach that level. A high-performing team achieves goals, communicates well, the team members work interdependently to accomplish their work, and your day-to-day involvement is not needed.

The way to develop a high-performing team is to give team

members both the technical and team skills they need. This is the training aspect of your job. You also need to help them through any performance issues or conflicts. This is the coaching aspect of your job. Eventually you want them to take over and lead themselves. This is the delegating aspect of your job.

Keep in mind that when you delegate, you do not disappear. You will always have to be involved with your teams no matter how high-performing they become. The amount of your involvement depends on what level you can get your team to. Delegating means letting the team take on responsibilities, but please be aware of what responsibilities you should always keep for yourself even when a team reaches an autonomous level. These include:

• Making sure the team is on target and will reach its goals. The team may even choose its own goals, but you are ultimately responsible for achieving the goals of your team.

• Taking the blame if the team does not succeed. I remember working on a team that flopped. The boss really let us have it for making, as he said, "such incredulous" mistakes. But we got our revenge. It just so happened that his boss was standing within earshot and heard what my boss said. In front of us, which probably was not a good management practice, the boss's boss said (and I will never forget these words), "As the manager of a team in this company, you are ultimately responsible for all the work that your team does. They get coached when they make mistakes so the same mistake doesn't happen again. But you get the blame!"

• Reminding the team of its goals and how they align with those of the organization—that is, sharing the big picture, or vision.

• Remaining the point of contact for other teams, departments, or individuals.

• Giving the team or a team member needed direction or support.

• Providing or obtaining the resources the team needs.

• 1 3 •

Team-Spirit Key #2: Open and Honest Communication

The second key to developing team spirit is open, honest communication between you and the team members. I always tell teams and their managers/team leaders to remember the three C's—constant, continual communication. The three C's avoid many future problems and they keep the team focused on its goals. It is a very proactive method for addressing issues before they become serious problems.

We can break open and honest communication down into six components. If you and/or your team can demonstrate these six components on a daily basis, you know your team has mastered the second key to team spirit.

The Six Components of Open, Honest Communication

• *It's timely.* When managers or team members notice or become aware of anything that one of the other team members is doing that may hurt or delay the team's work, they give feedback.

• *It's two-way.* Every team member feels comfortable communicating with the team manager, leader, or other team members, and the manager or other team members welcome this communication. The manager encourages two-way communication by emphasizing the team's importance, praising team members for communicating with her, and being available as much as possible for receiving communication.

• *It's valued.* All comments, suggestions, and opinions of team members and the manager are valued. Anyone's point of view can turn out to be the most valuable point for the success of the team. Individual team members are not put down for what they say. The communication is always presented in a way that maintains a team member's self esteem.

• *It's encouraged.* Some team members are a bit hesitant to communicate or share their views because they may be shy, think what they have to say is not important, or are responding to cultural cues. That is, they may feel pressure to not speak up if they disagree. Members of high-performing teams encourage their colleagues' input and encourage them to express their views and opinions.

• *It's delivered in an unemotional way.* Some team members get emotional from time to time. They may get upset about a delay or annoyed that a fellow team member is not doing his part. There is nothing wrong with emotions, and it is fine for teams members to say that they are angry or upset or distressed or whatever. In order to make the communication effective, however, team members must use the words to describe how they feel rather than demonstrate how they are feeling. Team members also have a lot of positive emotions, and they need to be encouraged to express those.

• *It's clear and understandable.* To have open communication, all team members need to understand what the message is. Their communication must be clear; precise; free from jargon or slang; and only use acronyms, abbreviations, words, or phrases that others can understand. They explain themselves. They give feedback to team members who are not being clear and understandable. A manager recently told me about her great strategy for developing clear and understandable communication among her team members. She had each team member bring to a team meeting copies of the last 10 business e-mails they received from other team members. Then the team reviewed the e-mails to see how clear, precise, and understandable they were. She said this got the message across beautifully.

While we are in our section on communication, I want to mention two communication situations that you need to be aware of as a first-time manager. The first has to do with a communication trap that teams fall into: group think. And the second one has to do with how you communicate with a virtual team.

Group Think

The success of a team depends on the team members' ability to share their thoughts, opinions, and disagreements in an open, honest, direct, and constructive fashion. A very dangerous communication behavior that often develops on teams is group think. It leads a team into bad or illogical decision making.

Group think happens when one or more team members begin to keep quiet when they have ideas or suggestions that differ from the rest of the team's thinking. This phenomenon occurs when a team is performing at a high level and the team members are getting along extremely well with one another. A team member may not want to upset the smooth operation of the team, hold up the team's progress, thinks he does not have as much expertise as other team members, fears the wrath of others, or does not want go against what he feels are the desires or the consensus of the team. This is dangerous because it suppresses ideas that may be valuable to the success of the team. In order to avoid group think, team members need to encourage everyone to say what is on his or her mind, even if it conflicts with the general consensus. Teams need to be educated about what group think is and how to circumvent its impact. As a manager, be on the outlook for certain signs that your team is in group think or about to get into it. Some of the more obvious cues include a dominant team player taking over, justification of poor decisions, feeling that there are no wrong decisions, not seeking the opinions of each other or of external or extended members, not being critical of other opinions, and coming up with few alternatives or only one to a problem.

The Case of Karol and Group Think

Karol joined her team about six months ago. She had worked on teams for years in her native county. However, the teams she was part of were work teams, where the team manager was in charge and made the decisions. Her current team is quite different. The team members make the decisions with the help of the manager. It has taken Karol some time to get used to this new way of working, but she now likes it and feels that she is an important member of the team.

A couple of weeks ago at a team decision-making meeting about the team's work processes, Karol had a suggestion for improving one of these processes. But she did not mention it. She thought nobody else would like her suggestion, and she did not want to have a different view from the other team members. Karol probably would have offered her thoughts if someone had asked her if she had any new approaches or innovations to the current process. Unfortunately, no one did. She knew as part of her team training on group think that she should have spoken up, but she did not. Perhaps if someone else would have given an improvement suggestion, she would have too.

Yesterday, at the team's weekly meeting, the team reviewed the work process that Karol had the suggestion for. It seemed that the process was not working too well and the internal customers were complaining. To Karol, it seemed that her suggestion would have avoided these complaints. Karol finally spoke up. She said, "I feel so bad. I thought of a way we could have avoided these complaints, but at our decision-making meeting I was guilty of group think. I thought everyone was happy with the agreed-upon process and I did not want to 'rock the boat.'" Then another team member spoke. She said she also felt that they would have problems with the process, but she too felt that she was the only one on the team thinking differently. Then a couple of other team members voiced the same idea. It was apparent that Karol was not alone here, but because of group think, Karol and her other teammates remained silent.

Communicating on a Virtual Team

Virtual teams are teams where the team members are not physically colocated. They are geographically dispersed, sometimes even around the globe. I once consulted on a nine-member virtual team. Two were in Australia, another two in Asia, one in North America (me), two others in South America, one in Africa, and one in Europe. The project was a great success, and what a fantastic cultural experience it was for me and hopefully for the other team members as well. Everything we have said about teams so far, such as the importance of developing team task skills, team process skills, and primary and leadership skills, holds true for virtual teams as well.

However, virtual teams face additional communication challenges. Working in different locations means team members miss out on the face-to-face contact that unquestionably helps build team spirit and increases effective communication. Two-way face-to-face communication is the most effective method of communication because individuals are able to pick up meaning not only through words but also through visual communication such as facial expressions and body language. Other communication challenges include language differences, accents or pronunciation issues, cultural differences, and time-zone barriers.

Technology makes virtual teaming possible, but technology is never a substitute for human interaction. And team managers need to be especially sensitive to any communication barriers. Even though it can be incredibly expensive, I encourage organizations, if at all possible, to bring virtual teams physically together occasionally. It is especially helpful to bring a virtual team together at the beginning of a project or when the team is first formed. This initial get-together creates a bond among team members and it builds trust. Without this bond and high levels of trust, virtual teams may perform adequately but it is unlikely that they will reach the participative or autonomous levels.

Many former first-time managers have told me that when their companies brought their virtual teams physically together, productivity improved tremendously. If the expense is too great for the organization, team managers must find every conceivable opportunity for virtual team members to communicate on a regular basis. I have found that net meetings work better than telephone conferencing. It is difficult for most people to focus for more than 10 minutes on a conference call, whereas people tend to be more engaged on net meetings. Also, briefer but more frequent meetings seem to work better.

And believe it or not, if team members put their colleagues' pictures and brief bios on their office walls, computers, or wherever, team meetings run much smoother and the team develops more of a team spirit. As the team manager, you should have each of your virtual-team members prepare a five-minute videotape introducing themselves. Then distribute these tapes to every team member. This helps team members become more comfortable and familiar with one another.

Virtual teams are the norm in many organizations today. And if you are not currently involved with one now, that will probably change for you in the near future.

Team-Spirit Key #3: A Supportive and Knowledgeable Manager/ Leader

The next key to developing team spirit is having a supportive and knowledgeable manager or team leader. This is especially crucial when the team is going through its initial development. Getting a first-time manager to become supportive and knowledgeable about teamwork is the responsibility of the team manager or leader herself, the team members, and the organization.

Let's begin with the latter. The organization has the task of re-cruiting individuals who can succeed in the team environment and the team-building role and then giving them training on manage-ment, leadership, and team skills. When organizations do this, it is much easier for the manager and her teams to succeed in their roles. Many organizations have training programs that accomplish this and others send their new managers and team builders to out-side programs.

The team members need to understand the manager's role in team building and learn to support her efforts. Team members need training as well. They need to learn how a team functions, how teams make decisions, how to communicate effectively, how

to work with the team leader, task and process roles, how to motivate each other and keep positive attitudes, etc. The current man-
ager/team leader can conduct this training if she has the skills and
training, or a specialized trainer can do it.

The third element in developing a supportive, knowledgeable
team leader is the team leader herself. She needs to communicate
her role to the team, what she expects from her team, and how
she is going to work with the team in order to make it a high-
performing team. She needs to use all of her team skills including
the task and process roles, and all of her primary and leadership
skills.

Say "We" Instead of "I"

The language a manager uses when talking with his team often
reveals his attitude toward teams. Sometimes just one word can
expose it.

For example, instead of saying, "I need to improve our relationships with our clients," say, "We need to improve our relationships
with our clients." Instead of saying, "You are in danger of missing
the deliverable date," say, "We are in danger of missing the deliverable date." Instead of saying, "Whose mistake was this?" say,
"How can we improve this?" Instead of saying, "Team, what are
you going to do about these complaints from the customers?" say,
"What should we do about these complaints from the customers?"
Instead of saying, "Our designs will not work," say instead, "We
have to do better."

A manager/team leader also needs to be cognizant of how she
is coming across nonverbally. Quite often a particular facial expression, an irate look, lack of eye contact, a roll of the eyes, or a sarcas-
tic tone sends a message to team members. We have to be very
careful that we are not allowing our unintentional communication
to take precedence over what we are saying. And as the communication experts tell us, communication is irreversible. Once you have
said something or communicated it nonverbally, you cannot take
it back.

Active Listening

Probably the best way to demonstrate to your team that you are a supportive manager is to be an active listener. I have never met a team member who does not like to be listened to. Listening is a pretty difficult skill, but active listening is even more difficult.

When you are listening, you hear sounds, words, and sentences and you try to make sense of what it all means. This is one-way communication. When you are actively listening, you are letting the other person, your team member, know that you understand or want to understand what he or she is communicating. You can do this by asking questions, putting the person's words into your own, encouraging the person to say more, or giving nonverbal signals that indicate you are following. Active listening is two-way communication.

When you are listening to your team members (or anyone else for that matter), try to focus on the message and not "who the person is" who is sending the message. You may have some preconceived notions about the person, and this will prevent you from actively listening. Train yourself to quiet your internal talking and only concentrate on what the other person is saying. Listen not only to the words but also the emotions—they may reveal more than the actual words do. But, on the other hand, try not to allow an emotional response to prevent your from listening to the message.

Years ago I was working with the CEO of a high-tech company in Silicon Valley. His VPs told him that he was not a very good communicator and especially not an active listener. I was coaching him on his communication skills when he said, "Gary, aren't there any communication acronyms that you can give me that if I remembered to use them, I could come across as an active listener?"

At the time, he was wearing a baseball cap. The cap quickly reminded me of the CAPS of active listening. I told him that I had the perfect acronym for him and that if he used it during his conversation he would automatically improve his listening by 50 percent.

CAPS forces you to be an active listener. The C stands for clarifying. During a conversation say something like, "Are you saying that . . ." or, "Let me make sure I understand what you are saying . . ." The A stands for acknowledging. Let the speaker know that you are still there and your mind has not drifted off. Say something like, "I am with you," or "I follow you." The P stands for probing. Ask relevant questions during the conversation. And the S stands for summarizing what you have heard or asking the other person to summarize what he or she said. To this day, the CEO uses CAPS and now gets very positive feedback on his active-listening skills.

Get Feedback

I highly recommend that a first-time manager, during the initial phases of team development, get feedback on how he or she is coming across to others. The person who gives the feedback can be someone who sees the manager in action a lot. It could be a colleague, another manager, or a team member. This individual has to be someone whom the manager highly trusts and feels is skilled in giving feedback. As teams become more participative and autonomous, they will take it upon themselves to give this type of feedback.

The Incongruent Message

I have also noticed that many first-time managers send confusing messages to their teams. They send one message with their actual words and a different message with their body language, facial expressions, or vocal tones. We have to avoid these incongruent messages. They cause much misunderstanding and a loss of team trust.

Team managers must also to be very cognizant of the nonverbal behaviors of their team members. Often these behaviors reveal much more about what team members are thinking and feeling than the words they are using.

How Can I Get Them to Trust Me?

Building a trusting relationship with your team takes time, and do not expect as a first-time manager that it will happen overnight. Trust is an integral part of building high-performing teams. If your teams do not trust you, they will not get to the participative or autonomous levels.

You build trust every day by demonstrating effective leadership skills. That is your most powerful strategy. You build trust by showing that you care and are concerned about your team. If you do not really care, your team will surely know it. You build trust by allowing your team members to make mistakes and learn from their mistakes instead of punishing them for their mistakes. If they get punished for making a mistake, they will never want to try something new or something that they are not already skilled in. You build trust by sharing your views, opinions, and even your own shortcomings. Your teams will bond with you more when they know more about you. And you build trust by giving your teams the freedom to act on their own as much as possible. This last one is the biggest sign of trust.

Sometimes, because of our own actions as managers and team leaders or because of the actions of the organization, our teams lose the trust they once had. For example, consider what happens if a team member says he would like to learn something new soon or take on a different role on the team. If you promise to accommodate this person but never do, he will lose the trust he once had in you. If your organization has been regularly communicating with the staff but without explanation it suddenly stops doing so, the organization loses the trust of its staff. When your team members lose trust because of what you or the organization has done, or both, there are five things you need to do:

1. Find out in specific terms why the team has lost trust. Was it something you or the organization did? What was the impact?
2. Have a plan for how you are going to regain trust even if it was not you who caused the mistrust. Acknowledge how the organization's action caused the loss of trust.
3. Demonstrate that you are making every effort to regain the team's trust.
4. Tell your management or organization how their actions caused a loss of trust and the impact their actions had on your team.
5. React quickly to losses of trust. Time works against you.

A supportive, knowledgeable team leader or manager needs to focus on two major areas when she is building her teams. She needs to focus on all five keys to developing team spirit. And she needs to focus on her own team-leadership development. One of the two is not enough. Both are essential.

Team-Spirit Key #4: Decision-Making Authority

The next key in developing team spirit and creating high-performing teams is sharing or turning over as much decision-making authority to them as they are ready for. When teams experience this demonstration of trust, their dedication and performance levels always increase. If the manager remains the sole decision maker, he will have a much harder time getting his teams to high-performing levels.

Teams, depending on their expertise and team skills, can make many decisions that affect their work. They can make decisions on time schedules, which procedures to use, methods for accomplishing their work, who on the team will do the presentation, what resources each team members needs, and even conduct performance evaluations of one another. It is really okay to let a team make a decision if it is qualified to do so. Remember, even though you are letting the team make a decision, it should have already had training in how to make team decisions.

Set Those Boundaries

You need to set boundaries and parameters for your teams in terms of what decisions they make and what decisions you make. You can set boundaries on anything that you feel the team is not ready to make a decision on or on decisions that there can be no debate or discussion on. For example, you can set boundaries on what the budget can be, deliverable dates, and what outside parties the team can and cannot get help from. And there might be no discussion on things like safety regulations and organizational, industry, or governmental standards and procedures that must be adhered to.

Readiness for Team Decision Making

Before a manager involves teams in decision making and/or turns decision making over to them, he or she should answer the following four questions to see if the teams are ready for the responsibility. The manager must be able to answer yes to all four questions.

1. Are the team members interdependent? If they are not, there is no reason for them to make decisions as a team. But individual team members can definitely make their own decisions about their own work products.

2. Are team members aware of their interdependence? If they are not, they are not ready to make decisions on their own or share the decision making with you. They need more development time and more training in team skills.

3. Are you willing to give the team the power it will need to make decisions and solve problems? If you are not, do you have valid reasons why? Remember, often the manager is the biggest impediment to teams making their own decisions. Additionally, even with the highest-performing teams there are some decisions the manager should make on his own even if the team is capable of doing so. Often there is a tight time schedule and no opportunity

for a team discussion. Or the manager has been told that he is to decide.

4. Are the members committed to the team and its goals? They had better be if you are letting them make important decisions. You want them to own these decisions and not be cavalier about them.

If you are not able to answer affirmatively to all of these questions, then you need to take a much more active part in making the important decisions that affect your team and the work that it is performing. Then, very gradually, begin to involve it in the decision-making process.

Modes of Decision Making

There are a few different decision-making strategies that you can use when you are developing your teams. The strategy that you use should depend on your team members' subject-matter expertise, their effectiveness in the task and process roles, and all of their other team skills.

With developing teams, get their input but make the decision on your own and then explain why you made the decision you did. There will be times when you have to make unpopular decisions. Sometimes the decision will be made for you, you cannot involve your team, and you know the team will not like the decision. When these situations occur, explain why you needed to make the decision the way you did, and then take the responsibility for making it. Or explain why others made decisions that the team needs to accept.

When the latter occurs, and it will occur quite often in most organizations, it is fine to say that you disagree with the decision, but then you need to say that you still support it and expect the team to support it as well. This is called no-pass-through management. It is communicating your support for decisions, policies, or procedures created by other people even if you do not agree with them. Hopefully you will be able to explain the decision and answer any questions the team may have to clear up any misunderstandings or misconceptions. At the same time, tell your team that you are doing everything possible to protect their interests.

With participative teams, you and the team members are making the decisions together. With autonomous teams, you are letting them make decisions on their own. The reason you let an autonomous team make decisions on its own is because it is qualified to do so, it probably knows more than you do technically, it has the team skills to do it, and because, at this stage in its development, it needs to. That is, if you do not let the team make decisions at this stage in its development, the team members will resent it and their performance will regress.

When we are talking about letting autonomous teams make decisions on their own, we are talking about decisions that affect day-to-day work. We are not talking about major decisions that only management can make. However, most autonomous teams could probably make decisions that affect the department or organization as well.

Consensus Decision Making

When a team makes a consensus decision, all team members agree to support the decision. Technically this process is called consensus without remaining objections. Consensus does not mean that every team member is convinced that a proposed decision is the best one possible. Consensus does mean, however, that every team member feels that he or she has been listened to and understood, and even if the team does not go with that position, each team member feels that the ultimate decision deserves his or her respect. If the decision does not work out, a team member would not say, "I told you so."

Consensus decision making is not easy. It would be much easier to make a majority decision by taking a vote; it would be even easier to make a minority decision by having one or a couple of people decide. This is why consensus decision making is one of the most important team skills once teams reach the participative and autonomous levels. It takes lots of discussion and open, honest communication, and it is a time-consuming process. Team members need to work through differences of opinions until they are resolved. The process can be draining and highly emotional as well. And for consensus decision making to work, all team members have to be engaged in the process. They need to be trained in the process as well.

There are three major benefits to consensus decision making. First, the decisions receive more sustained support because the team members all want the decision to work. Second, it builds team cohesiveness. Third, it creates better decisions.

There are also two dangers to be aware of when your team is engaging in consensus decision making. First, some team members may not be completely truthful about their opinions. Second, they may just agree with everything else that has been said in order to end the discussion and get it over with. Before you allow a team to engage in consensus decision making, you need to think about whether the team is ready to make decisions in this manner. Consider the following questions. You should be able to answer yes to all of them.

- Are the team members ready to put aside their own personal agendas for the betterment of the service or product that is the focus of the team?
- Is the team technically able (does it have the team skills?) and willing to engage in consensus decision making?
- Is the team well versed in all of the issues, facts, details, ramifications, etc. surrounding the decision that it has to agree on?
- Do you, the manager/team leader, agree to go along with the decision if you do not agree with it?
- Does your team see you as having an equal say in the discussion and not having more influence than anyone else?

Team-Spirit Key #5: Rewards and Recognition

The last of the five keys for developing team spirit is rewarding and recognizing teams for the valuable contributions they have made. When teams get rewarded for achieving their goals and working well together, they keep up their high-performance levels. When they do not get rewarded, the quantity and/or quality of their work products decline.

Can All Teams Be Motivated?

Unmotivated teams are common. They do the work because they have to, not because they really want to. Many first-time managers would say that you cannot motivate all teams. I disagree. I agree that it is not easy to motivate all teams. However, it can be done if we find the right motivators or rewards for each team. That is the challenge. First we have to find out through discussion what we could possibly do to motivate and reward a team. Then, and here is where it gets tough, we have to provide the motivators and rewards that work for the team. We also need to keep in mind that what motivates one team will not necessarily motivate another team.

How Do I Motivate My Teams?

There are two major ways to motivate teams. The first way is through rewards. Rewards are very tangible items and often have a monetary value associated with them. There are monetary rewards like bonuses or spot awards. There are gifts such as dinners, weekends away, or tickets to sporting events. It is important that these rewards are meaningful to the team members if they are to motivate them. Sometimes we give team members rewards that they do not appreciate, and these so-called rewards can backfire on us. They may even become demotivators for the team.

Rewards can be for the team as a whole or for specific members who have done incredibly well. You can even allow your participative and autonomous teams to select the individuals who will get the special recognition. They will be capable of doing it providing they have properly set up the criteria for determining who gets the rewards. I am a firm believer in rewarding both individual and team contributions at the same time. This type of reward system seems to work the best.

Then there are the more intrinsic motivators. The motivational experts tell us that these types of motivators, if they are the correct ones, last a long time. Intrinsic motivators have no direct monetary value. Examples include notes of appreciation from senior management, an article on the team's work and accomplishments in the company newsletter, positive feedback from the team manager or the actual people who have benefited from the team's work, or making the team the team of the month and giving the members valet parking or putting their pictures at the front entrance of the building. Providing an environment where our teams can achieve their goals, enjoy their work and their team interactions, work with autonomy, and be involved in the decision-making process is also an intrinsic motivator.

Let's Celebrate!

Too many first-time managers forget to celebrate team successes. For the sake of team morale, it is very important and necessary to do this. When the team reaches a milestone or achieves one of its goals, have a celebration. There are countless ways you can celebrate. Celebrations do not have to take a lot of time or be too costly to have a big impact. Often, just a 20-minute get-together from time to time, done spontaneously, goes a long way and gives you a big return on your investment. Celebrations also work very well for teams that are struggling. When you notice a small win for the team, have a celebration.

Adjourning

When a team has finished its project and is disbanding, the team manager should adjourn or end the team in a formal way. Just saying, "We are done," or "Thanks a lot for your hard work," just does not do it. Adjourning is another way to recognize the efforts of the team. It helps motivate team members to want to be on another team and to do well on that team. Adjourning is especially important for teams that have accomplished all of their goals and for team members who have developed a close working relationship with their fellow team members.

Here are a few suggestions for how to adjourn:

- Schedule a meeting to present the team's findings, solutions, recommendations, etc. and invite anyone affected by the team's results.

- Have your team develop tips for other teams. The tips can be on how teams need to work together effectively in order to achieve their goals. Your team will like doing this, and it will benefit other teams within your organization.

- Have one of the senior managers whom the team respects address the team and share how the team's work affected the organization or the greater community.

- Have the team determine what, if any, follow-up on the project needs to occur in the future.

- Have the team members share war stories with one another on their most memorable experiences, both positive and negative ones, of working on the team. Teams really love this one. When teams share war stories, they talk about difficulties with certain clients, conflicts team members were having, being on the 24th hour of a deliverable, or solving a problem that no one else was able to solve.

Reenergizing a Team That Has Lost Its Team Spirit

Some teams will develop all five keys of team spirit and reach a high-performing level, and then something causes them to lose their team spirit and not perform at such a high level anymore. This phenomenon is called regression. It can happen to the best of teams, including your participative and autonomous ones.

There are several reasons why a team might regress, and we have mentioned some of them already. They might be overmanaged, not have the latest tools to do their work as effectively as they would like, lose team members, get new team members, their goals might change, or the organization does not do well and there is job insecurity.

I left one cause off the list and I believe it is the biggest reason why high-performing teams regress: After weeks or months or years of steadily improving their skills and their ability to work interdependently, team members might feel there are no further growth or development opportunities for them.

If regression happened to a project team at the end of its project, there would not be a problem because the team is disbanding. But when it happens to an ongoing team, there is cause for alarm.

A team manager has a few options when regression sets in. She can try any one of these options or a combination of them. First, she can try to find additional assignments or projects that the team would be interested in. This would be the best option by far. This would definitely reenergize the team.

The second option is to talk with the team about the reality of the situation and own up to it as the manager. This option lets the team members know the manager recognizes what is going on. It often ignites the team to resume its normal levels of performance.

The third option is to do some benchmarking. Some very creative managers that I have worked with let their teams know how other organizations treat their teams and what their work environments are like. When their team members hear these stories, they are thrilled to be where they are. I once knew a manager who actually set up some site visits so her team could actually see what was happening in other companies. After these visits, they never complained again about what was happening to them. Now, if you find out the other organization's teams are doing better, forget about this particular option.

Option four is the most radical of all the options and most companies don't usually use it. A few companies realize that there are no additional learning or growth opportunities they can provide to teams or teams members who have reached a high level of performance. So here is what they do. If they cannot find the team members jobs or other positions in other parts of the organization, they help find them new positions outside of the organization if they choose to leave. Imagine how much team members would respect a company that did this.

There are many times when you will need to reenergize your teams besides when a team is in regression. When these times occur, you should follow four proven steps of reenergizing.

First, clearly define what the team's problem is and its causes. Second, develop an implementation plan to resolve the team's problems. Third, implement the plan. Finally, evaluate how the plan went. When the team members see you actively engaged in trying to help them and they see positive results, they will be reenergized.

Please remember that it is normal for teams to need to be reenergized. Do not feel guilty if it occurs. Many first-time managers do. Reenergizing teams is part of team development.

Closing Up

In this part of *The First-Time Manager's Guide to Team Building*, our focus was on how teams can develop the five keys to team spirit. Teams that have developed these five keys are high-performing teams. They have clear roles and expectations of each of their team members; they engage in open, honest communication; they are led by a manager or team leader is who is both knowledgeable of the work the team is doing and supportive of its efforts; they are involved in making decisions; and they get recognized and rewarded for achieving their goals. We also looked at how to reenergize teams and what to do when a team is in regression.

In part 4 of the book, we turn our attention to how we must hold teams and team members accountable for their performance and behaviors. We concentrate on what you need to do when your team takes on a difficult personality and how you can turn conflict into collaboration.

PART FOUR

Managing Challenging
Team Situations

• 1 7 •

Make Them Accountable!

Teams and individual team members need to be held accountable for achieving their goals and completing their work products and assignments on time. Rewards and recognition by themselves do not get teams and individuals to perform at high levels. Accountability has to be part of the equation as well.

I like to look at accountability as the last part of a five-part communication process. The first part is describing and explaining to the team members what is required of them. The second part is getting their understanding of what these expectations are. The third is the expectation that they will achieve the desired results and how they and the organization will benefit from achieving those results. The fourth part is having well-defined and well-communicated consequences for the team (or individual team members) if they do not get the expected results. The fifth part is actually implementing the consequences or holding the team accountable.

As a first-time manager you will need to hold some teams or individual team members accountable. Expect it and be prepared for it.

You may think that holding teams and team members accountable is too harsh. After all, throughout the book I have been touting creating a partnership with your team and letting it become as self-reliant as possible. However, if your team is not performing up to standard and you have tried everything and nothing has worked, you have no other choice but to hold it accountable. You need to do anything possible during this part of the accountability process to turn the team or any team member around. It is well worth the time it takes. It is always so much better to get your teams to want to do what they are supposed to do, instead of making them do what you want them to do. The work must get done and no team or individual team member can come above the needs of the organization.

Many first-time managers do not like to hold others accountable in such a direct manner. They want to be liked and are afraid they will lose the team's loyalty. Actually, in the long run, you will be respected more and have more loyal teams and team members if you do hold others accountable. Hopefully, and this is an extremely important point that I need to mention again, you and/or the organization must have tangible ways to hold teams and individuals accountable for not doing what they are supposed to. If you do not, good luck!

Holding teams accountable usually occurs on work teams and developing teams. It occurs much less often on participative and autonomous team. That's another reason for getting your teams to the high-performing levels. Additionally, team members on participative and autonomous teams have learned how to hold each other accountable and the manager does not need to get as involved.

• 1 8 •

Watch Out for Difficult Team Personalities!

In chapter 17 we focused on holding teams and team members accountable for their performance. We also need to hold teams as a whole accountable for their unproductive or destructive behaviors.

Every team, after a period of time working together, develops what we call a team culture or a team personality. A team culture defines the behaviors that the team values and which behaviors are acceptable and unacceptable. As team leaders, we always hope our teams develop productive cultures and value behaviors that facilitate accomplishing goals. Often, unfortunately, teams develop unproductive cultures. They take on these behaviors for many different reasons. Some of the many reasons include feeling that they are not getting the choice assignments or feeling that the manager is not developing or supporting the team.

A destructive team culture can become very powerful and often usurps the team's work and its relationships with the team manager or others outside of the team. It is critical to note that when teams develop difficult personalities, it is often not their fault but the fault of their team manager, the organization, or both. These destructive team personalities, if not addressed, will thrive. They are very threatening to the productivity and/or profitability of the organization.

When the Manager/Team Leader Is to Blame

A very tricky scenario occurs when the team manager has a personality trait, behavior, or habit (that she is often unaware of) that is detrimental to the team's success and the team adapts that trait or behavior for themselves. For example, consider a team manager who has a habit of speaking very loudly and all team members hear him when he is giving some critical or constructive feedback to one team member. Before you know it, many of the team members are doing the same, and a negative culture is created where team members criticize each other in front of others.

Other individuals from the organization, preferably the manager's manager, have to notice these types of destructive behaviors and make it their responsibility to give feedback and correct the situation. Sometimes managers or team leaders are too close to see what is happening on their own teams. To prevent this, many team-based organizations use people from other teams, departments, or organizations as process observers. They observe how the team is performing and how team members are interacting and then give feedback to the team.

It is unusual for participative and autonomous teams to take on difficult personalities. They have been educated and trained on how to recognize their own destructive behaviors and what to do about them once they occur. Therefore, here is yet another reason for getting your teams to those levels. Most destructive team personalities occur on work teams and developing teams.

The Seven Most Difficult Team Personalities

There are many kinds of harmful or detrimental team personalities or team cultures. These team personalities are readily seen at team meetings, and they are observable at many other times as well. In this chapter, I list seven of the most prevalent difficult team personalities. I also suggest what actions to take if one of your teams adopts one of these personalities and how you can prevent these team personalities from forming in the first place.

#7: The Winner-Take-All Team

They believe that every other team within the organization, or as a bit of an exaggeration, any other team that exists anywhere, is their competition. They have to win at all costs. They have to be the best team. They have to get the most kudos, the best projects, the best team members, the best rewards, have the best team leader, etc. Being the best at the expense of anyone else is their motto.

The Winner-Take-All team exists in a very competitive departmental or organizational environment. This type of environment emphasizes competition among teams too much. Instead, the department or organization should build an environment where teams are more cooperative with one another and realize they are all working toward the same goal: the success of the organization.

Another strategy that several organizations I have worked with use to prevent this high level of competition is to reward all teams or all staff members when the organization does well. That is, as long as all teams have made a valuable contribution to the organization. This creates a much more cooperative environment and greatly reduces competition among teams or departments. Be careful not to reward teams or individual team members who do not perform well. When we do this, we are sending the message that it is fine not to perform.

#6: The Tangent Team

What happens on a tangent team is that the team establishes a meeting agenda but does not stick to it. Team members always have something to say on unrelated topics or have their own personal agendas. They never get to the important issues the team is facing. They begin working on their assignments or projects and then lose their focus.

This personality type forms when the work, projects, or the problems that the team is charged with are too difficult to execute or are too unclear. You need to examine the team's skill set closely to see if it is capable of performing its responsibilities. Additionally, you need to review the clarity of the team's roles and goals.

I was speaking with a team manager a while back who had a tangent team. She said it was like watching a filibuster in action, where team members would go on and on about some trivial or unrelated topic to avoid doing the work. Eventually, and she admitted that it took her too long to realize it, she discovered that the new software programs the team had to use were new to them and they were embarrassed to admit that they did not understand them.

#5: The Social Team

Too many managers that I have worked with and some organizations that I have consulted in put people on teams because they work well together or have a nice mix of personality styles. Their skills and abilities seem to run a distant second. But they still hope that the work gets done. What happens in this scenario is that a social team forms. A social team is a team where everyone gets along well and enjoys the team experience, but the team does not accomplish the goals. Instead, the team spends its time socializing.

The core of the problem with the social-team personality is that the work is not emphasized from the beginning. That needs to be the priority. Observe a social team in its early stages and you will think it is the best team you have ever seen. No one is ever late to meetings, communication is outstanding, and everybody's energy and morale level is high. But come a little closer and you notice the work is not getting done. The team members eventually realize they are wasting their time and morale suffers.

Sometimes managers or organizations form teams to come up

with recommendations. If the team members were on these types of teams before and their recommendations were not used, the next time they are put on one of these teams, they will not take the work seriously. But because they need to remain on the team, they make the best of the situation. This is another example of how a team becomes a social team. To prevent social teams from forming, we need to have real goals that are meaningful to the team, and we need to have team members who have the technical skills to accomplish these goals.

#4: The Comedy-Show Team

Their focus is on having a blast. They are constantly telling jokes, pulling pranks, and never taking anything seriously. They are an extreme version of the social team. What usually happens here is that a few of the team members begin to joke around. Then others do the same. Then the team begins to get attention from others outside of the team for being funny and doing wild things. Before the team leader or team members know it, the behaviors have snowballed. The comedy-show team has to live up to its reputation. Joke telling and having fun are integral parts of what makes the team successful.

But when done to excess, the team loses focus. Many team members have told me that their teams turned into comedy teams when the work assigned to them was meaningless or unimportant or the work had a very low priority for the department or organization. Basically what they were doing was making fun of what the work of the team was supposed to be.

A member of a comedy team once told me about a team she was once on. It was called the logistics team. This team's mission was to analyze the amount of time conference rooms were used and who was using them. The idea behind the mission was to determine if conference rooms were used too much in general or too much by certain teams. If either was true, they were supposed to conclude that the work of those teams or the organization as a whole was not really getting done. The team was given three months for their study. When I heard this story I could not blame her team for turning into a comedy team.

#3: The Whining Team

Here, team members are constantly critical of the team's efforts, the efforts of each other, the project, their manager, the organization, the resources, the weather, the cafeteria, the day of the week, etc. They are looking for problems where often there are none.

It is rare for the whining team to give any constructive or positive feedback. Their members are very negative. Their attitude is a thorn to the team's progress and productivity.

There are a few main reasons why teams develop this negative approach. First, the culture of the department or organization is negative or the team has a negative manager. Teams pick up on the negativity around them, and before long they adopt similar behaviors. It is always worse when the manager is negative. This gives the team members even more of a license to be negative as well. If, on the other hand, the culture of the workplace were encouraging and motivating, teams would adapt those types of behaviors.

Second, teams whine when they are not listened to or their work is not appreciated. For example, if a team has spent weeks working on an innovative solution to a situation facing one of their customers, and, when they present the solution to their manager, it gets shot down without any explanation, the team becomes disillusioned and negative. It is a much better strategy for the manager to explain to the team why she thinks the solution will not work, get some additional ideas from the team, and encourage them to come up with another option.

Third, teams whine when we take something away from them. For example, if a team's budget for occasional lunches is taken away, or if a team used to be a partner in decision making but the new manager does not allow that, we open the door for complaining.

Fourth, change can cause whining. For example, if a major reorganization disperses members of a colocated team, the team members will miss the constant interactions they had. In order to reduce the impact that change has on a team, the manager needs to explain why the change is occurring (including any benefits to the change), explain the step-by-step process the change will take, and give team members time to adjust to the change. Listening to a whining team and letting it get its frustrations out is also helpful. But do not let these sessions go on too long. Set a time limit and move on from there.

#2: The Anti-Establishment Team

Their detrimental behavior is to separate themselves from the goals and mission of their team, department, or organization, and as individual team members to forget about their specific roles and responsibilities. Instead, they create their own work and their own goals.

Anti-establishment team members can be extremely productive, talented, and especially innovative when they set their minds to it. The problem is they are not working on what they are supposed to be working on. The number-one reason why teams take on the anti-establishment personality is because the team, too early in its tenure or development, is given free reign. The team manager's behavior becomes too hands-off too soon. Additionally, the team members are usually more knowledgeable or skilled than the team manager and they take that to mean that they can call the shots. And if the team manager lets them do it, they are well on their way to doing their own thing. In order to prevent this from happening, you have to establish specific goals for the team and hold the team accountable for achieving them.

#1: The Self-Destructive Team

This team wants the project that it is working and the entire team experience to just end and be over with as soon as possible. They will do whatever it takes to make this happen and they are usually very successful in making it happen. They purposely miss deadlines, give wrong data, come up with tons of excuses why they cannot do certain things, or literally stop working on whatever they are supposed to be working on. There are also many team-member conflicts that the team manager has a terrible time dealing with. Often the team members purposely create these conflicts to give the team leader a hard time. They no longer care about what the consequences are of the team failing.

What has happened here is that either the project was a bad one to begin with, it is going on forever, or the work is tedious and boring. Or the team has come to not like the manager or team leader or one another. Or it is upset with the organizational politics going on around them. The team just cannot take what is going on anymore and just wants to disband.

Most self-destructive teams get stuck in what many experts on team building call the storming period. They never get to establish team norms and never build any rapport with one another. They are constantly fighting, arguing, and nit-picking with each other. It is a very unpleasant experience. During this storming period the team leader or manager must be very strong and set up very clear guidelines on how the team will operate.

Early in my career I was on a self-destructive team, and I take the guilt for helping make it such a team. We were thrown together haphazardly and most of the 10 steps of team building were omitted. The team leader was in another part of the country and we rarely heard from him. We had a couple of team members with very strong personalities and they kept going at each other. And a lot of us, justifiably I think, kept blaming the department we were in for putting us into this situation. I can keep going on here, but I am sure you get the picture.

These are only seven difficult team personalities. There are many others.

Going from Conflict
to Collaboration

Conflicts are common in the workplace in general and on teams as well. As first-time managers, you should expect to have them with other managers, your manager, or your team members. You will also find yourself either resolving conflicts among your own team members or helping them resolve conflicts on their own. All I really mean by team conflict is a disagreement, different points of view, or different opinions between or among two or more team members or teams.

Welcome Conflict

When you have conflict on your team, welcome it. If team members are in conflict on how to improve a process, make the product better, provide a better service, or improve client relationships, you could not ask for anything better. You are lucky to have this type of conflict on your teams and you definitely want to encourage it. This is what is called productive conflict, or simply, good conflict. What usually results from productive conflict are better, new, or different solutions to the concerns and issues the conflicting parties are having.

But if your team members are having conflict around personality, work style, or differences in beliefs or values, then you are not too lucky. If one team member is critical of another team member's actions, behaviors, or appearance, this is unproductive conflict that must be resolved very quickly. If not, the team will become self-destructive. If you hear the following kinds of comments, then you know you have the bad type of conflict to deal with: "I do all the work around here, she hardly does anything," "I cannot figure out how he got on the team," or "Why does it take him such a long time to make a decision? It is obvious what we should be doing."

Causes of Team Conflict

There are several major causes of workplace and team conflict. Before you can resolve the conflict or help others resolve it on their own, you need to be aware of what is causing the conflict.

• *Intrapersonal—Conflicts Within Oneself.* A team member's internal conflicts often influence his or her working relationships with other team members. For example, consider a team member who needs her job and likes the team she is working with but is morally opposed to the product her team produces. Or consider a team member who knows that in order to develop a better working relationship with his colleagues he must spend more time with them during the workday but feels uncomfortable doing so.

• *Interpersonal—Conflicts Between Two or More People or Among Teams or Groups of People.* For example, consider a team member who knows he works very hard and contributes greatly to achieving the team's goals but at company-wide meetings the team manager or a team member takes the credit for his efforts. Or consider a team member who really believes she is a true team player who communicates well and cooperates with the team, but has a colleague who never communicates nor shares the vital information she needs to finish her part of the project.

• *Structural—Conflicts Innate to the Organizational Structure or the Work.* For example, consider a team member who, because of the nature of her team's work, never gets to work on other types of assignments. Or consider a team that, because of its high visibility and big-budget projects, always gets recognition from the CEO, whereas other teams that work just as hard or even harder never get that recognition.

• *Values/Beliefs—Differences Attached to Deep-Seated Emotions.* For example, consider a team manager who believes her team members should always be available to work on weekends if issues arise on team projects, but the team members prioritize their personal obligations over work on weekends.

• *Personality—Differences in Style and Behavior.* For example, consider one team member who is very organized, detailed, and systematic, but her colleague is last-minute, laid-back, and unorganized.

• *Perceptions—Differences in View or Perspective of the Situation or Issue.* For example, consider a team that attributes a problem to a lack of time to complete a prototype, but the customer sees the cause as a lack of skills and/or dedication.

• *Work Methods—Disagreements About Solving Problems.* For example, consider one engineer on a team who wants to use a current software application but his other team members want to try something new.

You Have a Choice

There are basically five different approaches a manager or team leader can use to resolve conflicts or help or teach others to resolve them on their own. They are creative collaboration, giving in, controlling, workable compromise, and avoiding. All are valuable and can be highly effective. The key to success is knowing how and when to use the different approaches. It is the manager's responsibility in the case of developing teams, and the responsibility of participative and autonomous teams, to learn each of these approaches and then be flexible enough to use any of them when the situation calls for them. It is also important for team leaders and high-performing teams to understand why they have chosen a particular approach to resolve a conflict. Figure 19-1 describes the five different approaches to conflict resolution and recommends when to use each one.

Creative Collaboration

As mentioned, the biggest benefit of conflict can be the willingness of both parties to come up with a solution that is better than their original solutions. Creative collaboration achieves this. It is a cooperative strategy where individual team members or teams agree to discuss one side of the conflict and then another side(s) of the same conflict with the expectation that all parties to the conflict are willing to see the conflict from the other perspective.

The motive for doing this is the betterment of the client relationship, team functioning, or the productivity/profitability of the organization. The parties are willing to either drop their initial positions and come up with a new alternative or fuse their differing points of view so that all sides to the conflict welcome the new resolution.

When collaboration seems to be the best way to resolve a conflict, have your teams and team members use this method. If they are unfamiliar with it, you will have to teach them how to use it. If they have trouble using it on their own, they will need your guidance. When teams use creative collaboration, they come up with great decisions or resolutions to their conflicts.

Creative collaboration definitely helps gets teams to the participative and autonomous levels. In fact, successful creative

FIGURE 10-1. WHEN TO USE EACH OF THE FIVE CONFLICT APPROACHES

Creative Collaboration—A Win-Win for Everybody

- When a long-term solution is required.
- When it is a bottom-line business issue and creative solutions are a must.
- When it is very important that conflicting parties talk at length with each other and see the conflict from the other side's point of view.
- When you want to end the conflict in a productive, constructive manner that results in increased motivation and commitment from both sides.

Giving In—Let Them Have It Their Way

- When the other party is more knowledgeable and knows best.
- When doing so will encourage the other party to give in on an issue that is important to you.
- When you want to build a positive working relationship with the team member and the issue is secondary to the relationship.

Controlling—Your Way or the Highway

- When a quick decision must be made and there is no time for discussion.
- When senior management has told you to resolve the conflict ASAP.
- When procedures, processes, regulations, safety rules, etc. must be enforced and there is no way they can be changed.
- When you are the only one with the knowledge or experience to make the decision.

Workable Compromise—Finding the Middle Ground

- When issues are somewhat complex, relationship building is important, and time is a factor.
- When the other party or team member will not let you get your way, or vice versa.
- When you will be somewhat happy even if you do not get everything that you want or expect.
- When both or one of the team members are not willing or are not able to engage in lengthy discussions.

Avoiding—Not Dealing with the Conflict at This Time

- When the issue is unimportant and it does not matter if the conflict is not resolved.
- When you want others to resolve the conflict on their own without your intervention.
- When you or the other team member or party to the conflict needs to calm down before either of you approaches the conflict situation.
- When others are in a better position to resolve the conflict than you are.

collaboration is a clear sign that a team has reached a high level of performance.

However, for this method of conflict resolution to work, individuals must believe in and follow certain guidelines.

Guidelines for Creatively Collaborating

- All parties to the conflict need to be open-minded and willing to listen to the opposing position.

- They need to realize that disagreement with another team member's position or point of view is not a personal attack on the other team member.

- Each team member is responsible for understanding and respecting different positions in the conflict.

- All team members involved in the conflict are willing to change their minds when all the positions have been discussed and when all information or materials have been reviewed.

- All team members agree that they will communicate, discuss, and work toward getting the best possible solution to the conflict, problem, or opportunity after all the information and materials have been reviewed and after all communication has taken place.

- All team members agree they are going to use a collaborative approach to resolving the conflict and their goal is a win for the client, team, and/or organization. If it is a win for any of those, it is a win-win for all of the team members involved in the conflict.

- The team members agree to express their emotions but not let those emotions interfere with the creative collaboration.

- They are aware that creative collaboration can take a long time and that much time and hard work is needed from all team members if they want to come up with a new or fused alternative to their current conflict.

Five Steps to Creative Collaboration

When the team members or parties to the conflict decide to use creative collaboration, they need to follow the creative-collaboration steps described in Figure 19-2.

Let's look at these five steps in greater detail.

Step 1—Express Your View of the Conflict and Invite the Other Team Members to Do the Same

Team members have the opportunity to present their views of the conflict. They should present their sides of the conflict using facts, supporting documents, past experiences, opinions from others, facts, information, etc. All of this substantiates their view of the conflict. When all sides to the conflict are presenting their argument, everyone needs to be willing to listen and make sure that all has been understood. Remember, in creative collaboration, all sides have agreed to be there and they want everyone to win. They are all interested in finding a great solution to their mutual problem. Thus, putting down or ridiculing a statement or opinion from a team member on the other side of the conflict is never part of creative collaboration.

FIGURE 19-2. THE CREATIVE-COLLABORATION MODEL

1. Express your view of the conflict and invite the other team members to do the same.

2. Get everything out.

3. See the conflict from the other person's perspective.

4. Agree on what, specifically, the problem/opportunity is.

5. Focus on the future.
   —Generate solutions (fluency).
   —Evaluate solutions (elaboration).
   —Select and implement a solution.
   —Evaluate the results.

Step 2—Get Everything Out

Often, what is behind many conflicts are other concerns or issues besides what is being openly talked about. Many times personality, perception, values, beliefs, work-style differences, methods on how to do the work, etc., are at the core of the conflict. It is imperative that team members tell the other side exactly what is annoying or troubling them, even if it is not central to the stated conflict.

Step 3—See The Conflict from the Other Person's Perspective

Here all parties summarize what they have heard the others say and at the same time are supportive of differing points of view. Only when all sides can do this will they be able to move toward a win-win solution. I have noticed that members of work groups or developing teams have a hard time listening to one another and understanding other perspectives. First-time managers are also guilty of this behavior. I think most of us are so interested in telling our own stories or just focusing on our own agendas that we find it very challenging to really see other points of view. It takes much practice and support for a team member to be able to see a conflict from another person's perspective, and first-time managers need to help their teams achieve this important skill.

Step 4—Agree on What, Specifically, the Problem/Opportunity Is

Many teams and managers that I have observed make the mistake of identifying the problem or opportunity at the very beginning of the creative-collaboration process and sticking to it even though it may not really be the true problem. It is better to discuss the conflict at length first and then state what the true problem is. By doing this, all sides have a much clearer picture of what the conflict actually is all about.

Some managers and team members get caught on whether to use the word *problem* or *opportunity*. A lot of managers feel it is quite important to be positive and never want to use the word *problem*. They prefer *opportunity* instead. Either one works for me. I think a team that is able to engage itself in a creative-collaboration process is already being extremely positive!

Step 5—Focus on the Future

It is vital to discuss the background of the conflict, what has caused it, and the differing perspectives on it. But as a first-time manager, you need to have your team members avoid the blame game or focus on the past. Your goal is to get them to resolve the conflict. Have them learn from the past but focus on the future. This last step of creative collaboration, focusing on the future, has four parts to it: generating solutions, evaluating the suggested solutions, selecting and implementing a solution, and then evaluating how well the solution worked in resolving the conflict.

Generate Solutions

The idea here is to get as many solutions from everyone as possible. This does not have to be done in one meeting. Many high-performing teams post the problem (or opportunity) on a wall or bulletin board or do it electronically. Then, during a week's time, for example, everyone can post or write down suggestions. This gives people time to think and come up with answers they may not have thought of during a quick brainstorming session.

Getting away from the typical brainstorming (which is often overused or not used well) also helps those individuals who are not comfortable with brainstorming. They may need time to think before they can generate solutions on the spot. There is an old expression that goes something like this: "Some people think to talk and others talk to think." I believe managers and team members need to be reminded of this expression often. Also, do not allow the solution-generation phase to go on endlessly. Having a time frame, such as the one week, is important or else this process can last forever.

Do not discourage wild or unusual solutions. In fact, you should highly encourage them. Often, your best solutions to the conflict come from them. And be careful not to allow your teams to stop at the first suggestion even though it sounds great at the time. Perhaps the seventh or eleventh suggestion will be the one that works best for them.

Evaluate Solutions

When the week has passed and you have noted all suggestions, the time has come to evaluate the suggested solutions. The team members (by now the conflicting parties have joined forces and it is impossible to tell who was on what side) look at the viability of each suggestion. This is the most difficult part of the collaboration process, and most teams, even your autonomous teams, may need your help or the help of an external member of the team.

Select and Implement a Solution

Now the team or the former conflicting parties choose a solution that has the full support of both parties and they develop an action plan for implementing it. The team or the former conflicting parties can also fuse together several different solutions. Once this is done, the team members develop an action plan for putting this solution into practice.

Evaluate the Results

Evaluating results is an often-overlooked part of creative collaboration. The purpose is to determine how well the solution worked. If it did, celebrate. If it did not, determine why not and go back to the drawing board. The conflicting team members may have to go through the collaborative process again. You or they may realize that collaboration will no longer work and that one of the other four approaches to resolving the conflict is appropriate.

Closing Up

In this part of the book we focused on dealing with and managing challenging team situations. You will always have these types of situations to face, so be ready for them. You will always have teams or team members who are not doing what they need to do. When this occurs, hold them accountable. Be aware that teams can take on difficult personalities and you need to notice these immediately and address them. Be aware that you, the team manager, can have difficult behaviors that the team adopts. You need to get feedback on how you are coming across.

A natural part of teamwork involves conflict. Conflict can be good, so encourage it. But when conflict becomes unproductive, it needs to be resolved. There are five distinct ways to resolve conflict, and they all work. You just have to know which method will work best in each situation and with the team members involved. Finally, when the opportunity arises and you feel your team is ready for it, teach or help your teams resolve their conflicts on their own so they come up with win-win solutions for everyone involved in the conflict, especially the organization. When that occurs, have them utilize the five steps to creative collaboration.

Part 5 of the book follows. It describes several team-building activities that will help your teams develop into high-functioning, high-performing teams.

• P A R T F I V E •

Team-Building Activities

•20•

Team Building as an Ongoing Process

As I have been saying throughout the book, managers and team leaders need to make the time to build a team. They also need to recognize that it does take time to build a team. It can take many months to do so. I estimate that on the average it takes 10 to 15 months to take a team from the developing level to a high-performing one.

Team building does not mean solely focusing on the team members' technical skills, which, obviously, are crucial for the team's success. Developing these skills is a major job that the first-time manager has to be very concerned about. Team building also emphasizes team skills—the skills involved in working together. How are the team members communicating with one another? Are they supporting one another? Can and are the team members taking on all of the task and process roles? What is the trust level among team members? Having team skills is also essential if a team is to become a high-performing one.

Team-Building Activities You Can Do

What follows are team-building activities a first-time manager or any manager can do with her teams without having any special training. The activities help facilitate team development and help weld a team into a cohesive unit. These activities are well-received by the overwhelming majority of teams I have used them with. I have used them countless times. Do not feel limited to the ones in this book. There are many others.

I have described in some detail how to lead each of these activities. The first-time manager or team leader can conduct them just as they are described here, or she can adapt them to her team or specific organizational environment.

The point is to do them. Team-building activities can be done at separate times, such as at retreats, regularly scheduled team meetings, or as part of the formal team-building education that teams and leaders receive from the organization. To be honest, they usually work better at team-building sessions or off-sites than regular team meetings.

As I have mentioned, I always encourage managers to take their teams off-site for a half day or a full day every several months. These are perfect times to do team building. It is always best for the agenda not to include too much about the actual technical work the team does. The focus should just be on team dynamics and how to get the team to function even better.

Each activity that follows has:

- When to use the activity
- The objective of the activity
- The suggested amount of time the activity should take
- The materials needed
- A description of how to lead it
- A debrief of the key learning from the activity

The Post-Its

When to Use

Do this exercise when the team is in its early stages of development, when there is not sufficient communication among team members, or when the team has become too serious and/or too task-oriented.

Objective

The purpose of Post-its is to have your team members feel more comfortable relating to one another on an informal basis and to be more relaxed when working with each other. This ice breaker will help interdependent team members work more effectively because when team members know a little about each other, they tend to work more productively together.

Time

About 40 minutes depending on the size of the group. Take about 10 minutes for the distribution of the Post-its and the writing of the items, 20 minutes for the go-rounds, and 10 minutes for the debriefing.

Materials

Packages of Post-it notes and pens and pencils.

Description

Have the team sit around a table or in an informal arrangement of couches and chairs. Pass out packs of Post-it notes of all colors. Ask the team members to take as many Post-it notes as they like (most individuals take two to five). Then ask each person to count the number of Post-it notes they have. Then say, "Each Post-it note represents something about yourself that you are pretty sure none of the other team members currently know." Have the team members write their information on their Post-its, one bit of information per Post-it. The information can be something about one of their former jobs, an interest of theirs, a favorite subject in school, favorite type of food, etc. Emphasize that they do not have to share anything that they do not want to. (The idea here is not to have them reveal their innermost thoughts, secrets, passions, and feelings.) Ask them to prioritize their items, with what they believe to be the most fascinating first. Then lead two or three rounds where each team member shares an item.

What usually happens during this activity is the team, when it comes upon a bit of information that it finds interesting, begins a conversation about it. I have never found a team member who was not able to come up with at least one item. Encourage any team member to add to his Post-its as the exercise is in play if he was able to think of only one item. Tell the team that items that have already been mentioned can be repeated. For the team member who has come up with many items, have them prioritize the top few.

There is a twist that you might want to try. Once everybody has written information on the Post-its, collect all the notes and read them out loud one at a time. Then have the team members guess who the author is and why they think so. At the end of the guessing, the team member who wrote the Post-it reveals her identity.

Debrief

When the activity has concluded, ask the team these questions: What was the purpose of the activity? Do you have a better sense of who your team members are now? How will the activity help you work more effectively as a team? Did anyone hold back information that they wished they had shared and would like to share now? Was there information about one of your team members that really surprised you? Why were you surprised?

The Original Game

When to Use

The Original Game can be used with any team to give it a creativity experience. It is especially helpful when a team needs to be more creative, when the team's work is becoming redundant, or when the team needs to get away from the daily grind and perhaps find a way to make its work more interesting.

Objectives

There are four objectives for the Original Game. The first objective is to see how creative a team can be. The second objective is to demonstrate to the team members that they can be creative. The third objective is to get the team to discuss what its process was for being creative and have it compare the process used in the game to the process it uses in its real work situations. And the last objective is to have the team members reflect on their team dynamics. That is, what communication was like, who participated, who did not, whether the goal was clear, whether the team had clear roles and responsibilities, who took on the task and process roles, etc.

Time

Forty-five minutes. Take 5 minutes for the instruction, 20 minutes for the development of the game, 5 minutes for playing the games (if you have divided your team into smaller teams), and 15 minutes for the debriefing.

Materials

Anything that is in the room or on the persons of the team members. Or you can bring in any sort of supplies or resources.

Description

Tell the team members that they have to develop an original competitive game that two or more people or teams could play just by using the materials from the tops of their tables. (You can substitute tables with desks, on their persons, or the floor, or a combination of any of these.) Say that the game does not have to be radically different from something that already exists. However, it should have an originality or uniqueness to it.

You will not believe how creative your teams will be with everyday familiar objects. The Original Game also works well if you divide your team into smaller teams and have a competition. If you do this, you will need to have a few categories for them to compete in. The categories can be: fun and excitement level of the game; clear, easy and understandable directions; the cost and ease of manufacturing the game; originality, etc. I recommend selecting three categories.

If you do the competition, you will need a judge to choose each category's winner and the overall winner. The judge can be one of the team members not involved in the competition, the team manager, or someone from outside of the team. Have the two teams decide beforehand what the winning team will get from the other team. The prize should be something symbolic like a standing ovation, the wave, or coffee service for the next few days. And if you divide your team into smaller teams, have the team experience each game before the judging begins. Also, if you believe the team has done a really great job with its game (when the team has not been divided) you can invite outsiders to play it. This action boosts the confidence and unity of the team.

Debrief

After the judges choose the winners, ask the team some questions like: Do you think you were creative and innovative in developing your original competitive game? What were some key factors that contributed to your creativity? Are you as creative back at work? If not, what are some of the barriers to creativity back at work and how can we reduce their impact? How do you think the team worked together? Do we work the same way back at work? Why or why not?

A Real Problem

When to Use

Do this exercise when the team is not talking about or confronting the real issues that are slowing its progress.

Objective

This exercise identifies and discusses roadblocks the team is currently experiencing, applies a problem-solving method to resolving those roadblocks, and gives teams an opportunity to make decisions. The exercise also introduces a novel way to brainstorm.

Time

Forty Minutes. Fifteen minutes to identify the real problems and 25 minutes to resolve one of them. Time frames are only suggestions. You know your team the best.

Materials

Easel and flip chart or whiteboards with markers.

Description

Ask the team to brainstorm a list of problems that the team is now facing or experiencing. You can use the traditional brainstorming method or a method called brain writing. In brain writing, each team member gets a stack of index cards and writes down as many problems as possible—one problem to a card.

Next, team members pass their cards to the right or left, one at a time. Any card they receive might spark an additional idea for them to write down. Brain writing is done in relative silence; that is, team members do not talk about what they are writing down. Collect all of the cards and post the answers. Brain writing works better than brainstorming when you have team members you think will not be willing to share team problems out loud.

Once the list is completed, the team members decide on which problem they want to discuss now and try to resolve. They can decide by prioritizing the problems and selecting the most difficult one, or they can select one that is of lower priority but, if resolved, would give the team a lift. If they can not decide, have them randomly select one to work on. It is best, even if they are at the developing level, for you to avoid deciding what the problem will be or to facilitate the discussion. Two examples of typical problems that teams come up with are deadlines not being met and team meetings not going well.

In order for this Real Problem to work, the team needs to be taught the problem-solving method. You also need to be prepared to give the team some parameters on what its decision can be and then allow it to make the decision on how to resolve the problem.

Debrief

Ask the team the following questions: Do you think we were honest in listing our problems or issues, or do you think there are others, perhaps even more important, that did not come up? If so, which ones? Was everyone working together to resolve the problem selected? Give examples of how we did so. How can we improve our brainstorming (or brain writing) process? Are you happy with the resolution to our problem? Why?

Well-Known Leaders

When to Use

Do this exercise when team members move into team-leadership roles and they need to know what leadership behaviors are appropriate and which are not.

Objective

The objective of this exercise is to identify the effective leadership behaviors that the team believes team members need when they take on team-leadership roles or the behaviors leaders should demonstrate. It also allows team members to reflect on their own current leadership behaviors.

Time

Approximately 30 minutes, depending on the size of the team.

Materials

Pieces of cardboard, string, adhesive tape.

Description

Have each team member think of a well-known leader who they believe is/was a very good leader. The leader has to be well-known to all members of the team. The leader can come from any arena of life: politics, the corporate world, popular culture, etc. Each person then writes the famous person's name on a small cardboard sign.

Instruct each team member to place his cardboard sign on the back of another team member. Make sure that the team member receiving the sign does not see the name of the leader written on it. The cardboard sign should have tape or a string attached to it so the team member can "wear" the sign during the activity. If a team member cannot think of a leader to write down, have a list of names available. Definitely do not give the team member the impression that the list contains names of leaders whom you feel are good leaders. Explain that it is just a list of names that some people would put into the good leadership category.

When all team members have names on their backs, give everyone a chance to read each other's backs. Next have the team gather in a circle. One at a time, each team member asks five questions about the leader on his back in order to guess that person's identity. The team member can only ask questions with yes or no answers. If she does not know the person's identity after five questions, then the team reveals the identity. Give everyone a chance to play.

Debrief

Ask the team the following questions: Do you agree that the person on your back is a good leader and if so, what characteristics made or makes the person a good leader? Which of these characteristics do you bring to the team when you are in a leadership role?

While everyone is answering the questions, make a list of leadership behaviors that the team admires. At future team meetings or team-building sessions you can refer back to the list and ask the team how it is doing with these leadership behaviors.

Continue debriefing with these questions: What leadership behaviors have we identified that are currently not present on our team and would be of great value to us if they were used more? What leadership behaviors have we identified that are no longer necessary for team members in a leadership role to use? How did you feel doing this exercise? How has it helped develop our team?

Team Temperature

When to Use

Do this exercise on a continual basis at all levels of team development to determine if all team members and the team leader are in agreement on how they are doing on team spirit.

Objective

This exercise determines how the team members and team leader rate the team on the five keys to team spirit. It also allows the leader and members to talk about how the team needs to change.

Time

Sixty minutes, including the discussion.

Materials

Team Temperature questionnaire and scorecard.

Description

Explain to the team that you want to get a reading on how well the team feels it is demonstrating the five keys to team spirit: Clearly defined roles and responsibilities, open and honest communication, a supportive and knowledgeable manager, decision-making authority, and rewards and recognition.

First, ask the team members to complete the Team Temperature questionnaire on their own. Once all team members have done this, share the results and engage the team in a discussion on the ratings for each of the five keys. Members can fill out the questionnaire anonymously or you can ask for names. This decision depends on the trust level the team currently has. If it is very high, then team members will speak openly and you can do the questionnaire together or have team members write their names on it; however, if trust is not quite there yet, it is better not to ask for names so you can get more accurate results.

I have included a sample Team Temperature questionnaire. You may want to add or delete items to make it more relevant to your team. Do the scoring on your own, or together with the team, or let a team member or two do it. Then the most important part of the activity comes—the discussion of the results and what you and the team can do if the results are not up to par.

The Team Temperature Questionnaire

This survey measures your opinions on how our team is doing on team spirit. Using the scale below, circle the number that corresponds with your assessment of each statement about your team. Add the points for each section and place the results in the spaces provided. A score of 25 is the maximum for each category. The maximum overall score is 125.

Scale

5—Definitely True

4—Usually True

3—Somewhat True

2—Usually Untrue

1—Never True

Clearly Defined Roles and Responsibilities

1. Everyone knows his or her role.	5	4	3	2	1
2. All know and understand the team's role.	5	4	3	2	1
3. Team members understand how their roles fit into the goals of the team.	5	4	3	2	1
4. Everyone on the team knows the roles and responsibilities of each other.	5	4	3	2	1
5. Having clear roles is important for a team.	5	4	3	2	1

Roles and Responsibilities Score: _____

Open and Honest Communication

6. Our leader consistently lets us know how we're doing on meeting our goals.   5 4 3 2 1

7. We work together to set clear, achievable, and appropriate goals.   5 4 3 2 1

8. If the team doesn't reach its goal, we are more interested in finding out why we failed rather than in blaming team members.   5 4 3 2 1

9. We give feedback to team members whom we feel are not doing their part.   5 4 3 2 1

10. Our team leader is open to our feedback.   5 4 3 2 1

Communication Score: _____

A Supportive and Knowledgeable Manager

11. The manager has enough technical knowledge and experience to guide us in our efforts.   5 4 3 2 1

12. The manager develops all of our skills and is supportive of our needs.   5 4 3 2 1

13. The team manager tries to give us ownership of the work and does not take the credit for it.   5 4 3 2 1

14. Our manager keeps everyone up-to-date about what is going on in the organization.   5 4 3 2 1

15. The manager is well-respected by the company.   5 4 3 2 1

Manager Score: _____

Decision Making

16. Outsiders would describe the way we make decisions as productive and constructive.   5 4 3 2 1

17. We work together to make decisions rather than ignore them.   5 4 3 2 1

18. The team encourages every person to be open and honest, even if people have to share information that goes against what the team would like to hear.   5 4 3 2 1

19. Our team believes everyone has something of value to contribute to the team discussion and our opinions are vital to team success.   5 4 3 2 1

20. Consensus decision making is very good.   5 4 3 2 1

Decision-Making Authority Score: _____

Rewards and Recognition

21.	The team has the skills and motivation it needs to get rewarded for its efforts.	5	4	3	2	1
22.	Team rewards make sense to the whole team.	5	4	3	2	1
23.	There is a good match between the capabilities of team members and their recognition.	5	4	3	2	1
24.	We clearly understand what the team has to do in order to get rewarded and recognized.	5	4	3	2	1
25.	Team members give recognition to each other.	5	4	3	2	1

Reward and Recognition Score: _____

Scoring Instructions

Average the team members' scores for each of the five key areas. Put these scores in the first column of the Scorecard. Then fill in the team leader's score and the difference between the team and the leader scores. A score of 20-25 in any category is near perfection and the sign of an incredibly high-performing team. A score of 16-19 denotes a team is doing well in that category but can do better. A score of 12-15 denotes a team is in the developing mode, and a score below 12 signifies deep problems with the team's functioning.

Debrief

Have a broad discussion on what the scores mean. Then ask a few questions. What areas do we need to improve in? Where are our strengths? How would you analyze any gaps between the team leader and the team? What other items, not mentioned in the survey, are sore points (strengths) for us?

QUESTIONNAIRE SCORECARD

Five Keys to Team Spirit	Team Member's Results	Leader's Results	Difference
Roles and Responsibilities			
Open/Honest Communication			
Supportive Manager			
Decision-Making Authority			
Rewards and Recognition			
Total			

The Unsighted Square

When to Use

Use the Unsighted Square to emphasize the importance of effective team communication and leadership and when a team is having communication or leadership difficulties.

Objective

In this exercise team members experience a communication process and then relate the experience back to how the team communicates on a regular basis. Team members gain insight into what effective team communication entails.

Time

Sixty minutes: 10 minutes to prepare the team; 25 minutes for the activity; and 25 minutes for the discussion.

Materials

Index cards, a 100-foot rope, one bandana (blindfold) per person.

Description

The Unsighted Square is the best team-building exercise I have ever used. The insight that the team members get from it is uncanny, and they will refer back to it for months to come. It really demonstrates the team's current communication strengths and gaps. There is only one concern you may have with using it—you need a large indoor or outdoor space to do it in. The perfect time to do this activity would be at your off-site.

There are two things you need to do to prepare for the activity. First, designate at least one team member to be the observer, who will give feedback after the activity is completed. Have that person debrief the activity as well. Secondly, prepare seven five- by seven-inch index cards. Write one of the following items on each index card. Write very clearly and large.

- The rope must be fully extended.

- The rope is 100 feet long.

- Everyone must have at least one hand on the rope when we are finished.

- We have to form a perfect square.

- The time limit is 25 minutes.

- Blindfolds must be worn until we are finished—no peeking allowed.

- Someone will be watching us, so do not worry about falling or about your safety.

Take the team to the space where you will do the team-building activity. Tell the team members they will be engaging in an activity that will tell them a lot about how teams communicate and behave. Do not reveal any more information. Distribute the index cards to seven different team members and tell them they must memorize what is on their cards. Give them 30 seconds to read their cards and then collect them. Then ask the team to put on their blindfolds. Tell the team members not to worry about their safety because someone (perhaps you) will be watching their every move.

Find out beforehand if anyone is uncomfortable wearing a blindfold—you can have that person take on an observer role. Some team members will be wearing eyeglasses. Either collect them or have the team members put them on over their blindfolds (it makes for a great photo opportunity). After everyone is blind-folded, hand one team member the rope. Then do not say anything else during the activity except for giving time updates every five minutes or so and if you notice a safety concern or a blindfold not fully on.

What usually occurs next (though I have unfortunately seen some teams never do it) is that the team members with the index cards tell everyone what was written on their cards (do not ever tell them to do this). You will really be fascinated by how the team goes about solving this problem of making a perfect square, unsighted.

Either you or one of the observers needs to watch out for any safety issues. I suggest using a space that has no obstructions in it and where the ground is level. Also, the space should be as private as possible without any "outsiders" watching. Outsiders will make the group very uncomfortable either during or after the activity, or both.

You can be somewhat flexible with the time. For example, if the team seems like it is getting it and there are only two minutes left, you can ask the team if it wants another five minutes.

When the time is up, tell the team members to remove their blindfolds so they can see their results. They have accomplished their task of solving the Unsighted Square if they have formed a perfect square (it doesn't have to be 100-percent perfect), all team members have at least one hand on the rope, and the rope is fully extended. Give the team a few minutes to talk among themselves or as a large group before the debriefing. They will probably be very excited and most will have a lot to say before they can focus in on specific questions.

Debrief

Debriefing is always very important and the debriefing for this activity will be a very valuable learning experience for the team. I suggest beginning this section with a go-around. Have each team member say whatever he or she wants about the exercise. Then have the observer or observers give their feedback on what they noticed. Then, ask the following questions (if they have not already been discussed). These questions are just suggested ones. Based on how the team performed, you will probably have additional or different questions.

- What worked for the team? What did not work?
- Did everyone feel he or she participated? If not, why not?

- What was leadership like? Who was the leader? Was she effective?
- What was communication like? Was it effective? What could you have done differently?
- Compare communication during the activity to communication on the team during regular work time. What are the differences?
- What did you learn from the Unsighted Square that will improve our working together?
- What did you learn about team dynamics from this exercise?
- What insights did you get about yourself from this exercise?

Closing Up

I have shared many team-building activities that you can try with your teams. Your teams will find the exercises fun and challenging. They can be a bit risky as well. That is, team members will reveal things about themselves that they may not have shared before, and they will receive feedback that they might not want to get. It is important that you explain why you are doing these exercises. Also, do a very thorough debrief after each one. People will gather insights during the exercises, but the message or objective of the exercise gets firmly planted during the discussion and the debriefing.

· 2 1 ·

Conclusion

Becoming a first-time manager brings you much power and influence with the teams that you manage or will be managing. You have a choice on how to use this power and influence. You can decide that you are going to be the one in charge, the one who makes all the decisions and closely directs and supervises each of your team members. If you manage this way, using what we call your positional power, your team members—if they want to be there—will do as you say. Using your new positional power will get you results but only over a short period of time. Additionally, high-performing teams rarely develop when a manager only uses his positional power.

You are better off using your personal power. You develop this power over time, and it is given to you by your team members. When you have this power, your team members will readily do what they are supposed to because they want to. You will get their commitment and change their attitudes so that they work hard not only for you or the organization, but especially for themselves.

You develop personal power by being a manager who has class. A manager who has class wants to develop his teams so they become as high-performing as possible. Teams can easily recognize a manager who has class.

- A manager who has class builds a team spirit by clearly defining roles and responsibilities, encouraging open and honest communication, providing the knowledge and support the team needs, involving the team in the decision-making process, and rewarding and recognizing its achievements and accomplishments.

- A manager who has class knows the differences among all of the team structures—work group, developing team, participative team, and autonomous team.

- A manager who has class uses the three factors of team life to determine which team structure would serve the needs of the team the best.

- A manager who has class tries to get the team to the highest level of performance possible.

- A manager who has class avoids overmanaging and undermanaging.

- A manager who has class knows the conditions necessary to develop a team-based organization and knows that one of the conditions is the manager's attitude.

- A manager who has class is willing to develop new skills, including primary skills and leadership skills.

- A manager who has class does not send mixed messages about the importance of teams and would never punish a team that is doing well.

- A manager who has class reaches the third phase of change: starting over.

- A manager who has class builds teams by closely following the 10 steps of team building.

- A manager who has class leads effective meetings and teaches others how to run their own effective meetings.

- A manager with class recognizes that teams will regress and does everything possible to get them back on track.

- A manager with class holds teams accountable for doing what they are supposed to do.

- A manager with class is very alert to the different difficult personalities that teams can take on and has specific action plans to prevent this from happening.

- A manager with class is aware of his or her own behavior and how that behavior can be detrimental to a team's success.

- A manager with class recognizes that teams and team members will have conflict and embraces conflict as beneficial for the team's development.

- A manager with class knows how and when to use the five different approaches to managing conflict.

- A manager with class teaches teams the creative-collaboration model for turning conflict into collaboration.

- A manager with class constantly focuses on how to enhance team dynamics and uses many different team activities to accomplish that goal.

- A manager with class knows that team building is an ongoing and continual process.

- A manager with class knows that you do not "do" team building once and then never do it again.

- A manager with class really cares about the team and understands that teams will really know if she cares.

If you have class, you will do incredibly well. Good luck.

Index